For my husband and my three wonderful children,
Aubrey, Addison and David Jr.

ACKNOWLEDGMENTS

"With God, all things are possible." Mathew 19:26

I would like to thank the following people for their contributions and support in making Stretch Marks become a reality: My Husband, David and my friends John and Diana Burton.

A big thank you to my children Aubrey, Addison, David Jr. and my Godchild Ashlyn for their patience, inspiration, support and most importantly for teaching me how to live a full and enriched life.

Thank you to my mom, Yvonne, who continues to teach me how to make sense of my world by getting organized, prioritized and then taking action.

Thank you to my dad, Ernie, who continues to believe in me.

STRETCH MARKS

A Mother's Journey To Awareness

Crystal

Crystal Horton

Kayla,
You are a GENIUS!
Love You
xoxo
Crystal :)

STRETCH MARKS
Copyright © 2015 by Crystal Horton

ISBN 978-0-692-62597-2
Printed in the USA
Cover Design by Stan Holden, The Looney Bin, Creative Agency www.TheLooneyBin.com

I wish to also thank personally the following people for their contributions, inspiration and help during the creation of this book:

Ben & Shalah Aguilar, Bernice & Fred Trujillo, Joe & Rufina Baca, Dorothy Aguilar, Connie Espinoza, Candice Horton-Archuleta, Rachelle Mriglot, Lynda Pauley, Sandra Bankston, Amanda Lira, Eufrasia Neely, Juanita Aragon, Megan Trujillo, Jeni & Cameron Vincent, Sarah & Jake Stone, Kasey Atkinson, Jody Reeser, Arturo Jaramillo, Shyla Prijatel, Kristen Hoover, Shan White, Charleigh Vigil and Ryan Balchuck.

CONTENTS

FOREWORD

When I first heard the title of Crystal's new book, "Stretch Marks" I smiled because it so aptly describes Crystal's journey as a parent, spouse, and entrepreneur. As I read her initial manuscript, I found myself laughing, crying and experiencing one aha moment after another.

Crystal has a unique way of turning calamity into triumph and exposing the everyday trials of parenting for what they truly are ... opportunities to learn and grow and become more understanding, compassionate people.

As a coach and family strategist, Crystal offers her client's creative, effective, parenting strategies designed to help them navigate through today's fast paced parenting environment. Having spent time with Crystal and her family, I have watched how she and her husband David engage and encourage their family in fun, cooperative ways that truly foster a team spirit.

Throughout the pages of Stretch Marks, Crystal offers the reader a plethora of humorous examples of those moments when her attempts at parenting simply "went south" and what she learned in the process. It's in these moments that her parenting humility shines at its very best.

Whether you are just starting out on your parenting journey, or you have been at it for many years, Stretch Marks is guaranteed to make you smile and give you hope. I highly recommend Crystal as a family strategist. Crystal is gifted at helping her clients find effective solutions to everyday parenting challenges.

Stretch Marks is a must read!
John Page Burton
Author, Wisdom Through Failure and Knowing Sh#t from Shinola

"My stretch marks have become a daily reminder that life is truly a gift."
-Crystal Horton

INTRODUCTION

The loss of a child is something no parent wants to go through. Our son, Ian, was twenty-two weeks old when he died.

One of my favorite memories is how Ian held his right hand over his heart. His palm was facing towards me, his fingers tightly touching, revealing every line in his tiny hand. This beautiful hand gesture brought a smile to my face and provided peace to my soul. His eyes, curly hair and the way he crossed his little arms brought joy to my heart. The way his feet swayed to the right from his ankles is the same way his daddies do, simply perfection. How could such a person so small have to leave this earth so soon? God must have needed an angel, but why Ian? Why did it have to be us?

Two days after Christmas, Ian died. We learned the true understanding of hello and goodbye. My husband and I discovered God together. Our bond grew stronger spiritually, even though we had grown up in different religious settings.

At one point during my grieving, all I wanted was to get

back to my pre-pregnancy weight. I thought if I could do this everything would go back to normal, to the way it had been before Ian died, and it would be as if nothing bad had happened. The pain would disappear. I had become delusional. No matter what I did, it wouldn't bring Ian back.

When the time came to pack Ian's belongings, my grief became unbearable. My husband and I cried together, our bond continued to grow closer. Knowing we only had each other brought comfort and healing to our sadness.

My husband and I had married a few months prior to the death of our son. We were grieving as newlyweds. Years later, I realize the foundation of who we are today as a couple, as individuals and parents was formed during those twenty-two weeks.

My stretch marks have become a daily reminder that life is truly a gift. Today, my husband and I have three healthy children. On this journey, we have grown together, formed a strong bond in our relationship and with our children. Ian will always be an enduring part of our family and has become a symbolic meaning for how our family lives today.

MY DISCOVERY

During the process of writing Stretch Marks, I discovered something great about myself and my parenting. I originally began writing as a way to help heal my grief from losing my grandmother. We had talked weekly and had become great friends. She was my mentor and taught me so much about raising a family. I began writing because I didn't want to forget the many lessons she taught me. The more I wrote the more I realized how the traumatic experience of my son's death carried into my daily interactions and parenting patterns.

The more I studied healthy parenting patterns, the easier it became to grow as a parent. As I faced my fears, I demolished them and began thriving again. Today, I view life from a completely different point of view and absolutely love every second of it! In sharing the imperfections of my stretch marks, my "tiger stripes" remind me that I'm a survivor of change. This positive change will carry with me knowing that life is truly a gift.

I've discovered the key to a healthy relationship comes from effective family communication, self-awareness and time management. Below, are some of the things I've learned during my research writing Stretch Marks.

Family Communication:

My husband and I are the foundation of our family. We laugh together, we support each other, we talk it out and we often compromise before moving forward. In short, we are a team. As parents, we understand that our verbal and nonverbal cues set the tone in our home. The more we are present the better it is for us and our children.

Self-Awareness:

Writing something this personal has been very humbling. I have learned to live a "new normal," by asking for support from family and friends and to celebrate in the memories. My hovering instincts kicked in to protect my fears but the more I wrote the more I became aware of the obstacles I was facing because of my avoidance. I made a vow to become a better me not only for my well being but for the well being of my family. I'll admit it was tough but the more I practiced change the easier it became. I learned that when I resist something the tougher I am on myself which translates into my parenting.

Time Management:

For our family, balance is recognizing what's a priority and what can wait. Planning ahead minimizes the amount of time we waste on unnecessary tasks and provides each family member the opportunity to contribute, learn something new and be ready to go. Single-tasking, delegating and expecting the unexpected helps us to thrive even when we have an overloaded calendar and endless to-do list.

Writing Stretch Marks allowed me to truly grieve the death of my son and also become a healthier wife and mother during the process. The love I have for my family grows stronger each day. There are books I would have never read, seminars I wouldn't have attended and people I would have never met if it weren't for writing Stretch Marks. Who I've become today has been greatly impacted by the research I conducted during this wonderful writing journey. My hope is that you enjoy reading Stretch Marks as much as I've enjoyed writing it.

Crystal Horton
Pueblo, CO 2016

"Defining family values shows the pride and responsibility parents take for how they want their children to grow and flourish."
-Crystal Horton

TRADITIONAL AMERICAN FAMILIES

The traditional American family of the 1950s seemed quite innocent compared to today. Mothers seemingly dressed to the nines, had perfect hair, wore high heels, baked cookies and had dinner ready when their husband arrived home from work. Families sat together during dinner and engaged in conversation. On the surface, there seemed to be a great deal of peace and harmony within the family unit.

In the mid-1960s feminism arrived. Women like Gloria Steinem began advocating women's rights and demanded political, social and economic equality to their male counterparts. Thus, began a shift in family dynamics.

In the 1970s, the women's movement gained more steam. Mothers continued to take on the role as primary caregivers but were also beginning to enter the workforce in larger numbers, which was the beginning of "the balancing act."

In the 1980s more and more women began working outside the home. Parents began sharing more and more responsibilities, and children started becoming more self-sufficient.

By the 1990s, the traditional American family was adapting to the changing times. Parenting books were popular. Both husbands and wives worked outside the home and children learned how to bake cookies on their own.

Fast forward to today. We see many different family structures, coping, surviving and thriving. Moms are rising through the corporate ranks, dads want more time on the golf course and children are living a seemingly virtual life in the digital revolution. Societal norms continue to dictate that the majority of moms are the primary caregiver. Entrepreneurship is at an all-time high, and the dual family income has become the new normal.

In short, over the last 50 years the family dynamic has changed dramatically. Families are striving to find balance. This change has brought about an array of complexities. Researchers who study the structure and evolution of American families have noticed an emerging theme.

In a recent New York Times article, Natalie Angier explains their hypothesis. "American households have never been more diverse, more surprising, more baffling. Families, they say, are becoming more socially egalitarian over all, even as economic disparities widen. Families are more ethnically, racially, religiously and stylistically diverse than half a generation ago.

In increasing numbers, blacks marry whites, atheists marry Baptists, men marry men and women marry women. Democrats marry Republicans and start talk shows. Good friends join forces as part of the "voluntary kin" movement, sharing medical directives, wills, even adopting one another legally.

Single people live alone and proudly consider themselves families of one and are more generous and civic-minded than so-called "greedy marrieds."

The word "family" comes from the Latin word servant. A devoted family that is helpful, supportive and a follower of one another is a thriving American family.

The definition of family is ever changing. Below are some questions to reflect on as you create your definition of family.

1. What does the word love mean to you?

2. What values are important to you?

3. What's your parenting style?

4. What are your goals as a parent?

5. What is your family mission statement?

DEFINING FAMILY VALUES

My grandparents would routinely say "A family that prays together stays together." Through this continuous affirmation, my grandparents, my mom and my aunts formed a bond of commitment toward family. Family values passed from one generation to the next, providing me with an understanding of how to form a common purpose with my own family. A family that contributes to a common purpose provides affection, support and emotional strength toward one another.

Susie Duffy, a marriage and family therapist, defines family values as "the foundation for how children learn grow and function in the world." Ideas passed from one generation to the next sets an example of how to thrive with teamwork, love and play. These are core lessons for family beliefs and understanding. Family history provides a roadmap for understanding how family values form. Talk proudly about your family history and show pride in where you came from. If values are not clarified, parenting can be confusing, frustrating and imbalanced.

Consider writing a mission statement that defines your core values. Good friends of mine, Jeni and Cameron, have their values framed and posted on a kitchen wall. "In this home we are obedient, kind, caring, compassionate, independent and responsible."

A few examples of family values include social, political, religious, work, moral and recreational values. Share your thoughts with your children. Be open-minded and understanding that their opinions will change as they grow, and they may not agree with yours. Create a positive environment. Welcome new opinions. An environment like this will encourage children to speak up without fear of judgment.

Defining family values shows the pride and responsibility parents take for how they want their children to grow and flourish.

PARENTING PARTNERS

A parenting partner is an individual in a parent's circle of influence believed to be a good role model for their child. "It takes a village to raise a child" so choosing members of the village wisely can have a profound impact on the child's development.

"Roger Collantes, the author of Beyond Survival: How To Thrive Amidst Life's Inevitable Crisis, states that "ninety percent of a child's critical brain development happens within the first five years." Children form and carry their childhood lessons into adulthood.

Studies have shown as a child grows up they begin viewing family members, friends, daycare providers, teachers, and coaches as role models. Have you ever asked a child what they want to be when they grow up? Their response usually identifies an adult they admire. Parenting partners are people we trust our children with when we are not around. These partners encourage or discourage children.

Below are some questions to consider when choosing a parenting partner:
1. What are your beliefs, values and aspirations?

24

2. What is your parenting philosophy?
3. What characteristics do you seek in a role model for your child?

Are these three questions in alignment with your spouse's parenting philosophy?

Here's a recent example. I was at the school playground when a child ran excitedly towards his uncle and began explaining the science project he would be working on when they got home. The boy's uncle responded with encouraging words and offered to talk with the science teacher before they left, in order to better understand the project. At the other end of the playground, a little girl ran excitedly towards her grandmother trying to explain the same science project. Her grandmother passionately exclaimed, "homework is worthless." Which parenting partner would you choose?

Choosing parenting partners with similar interests and goals helps ensure the child is raised in an environment that will encourage continuous growth. Our values and beliefs will help our children make better choices.

TABLE TIME

Dinner is my favorite meal of the day. It's not about the food rather it's about the opportunity for the five of us to sit, pray and eat together. Table time allows us to tell stories about our day, the challenges we faced and we can laugh together.

Dr. Laura Markham, the founding editor of Aha! Parenting, explains that "families who eat together also talk more, which helps them stay connected and build better relationships." Our family breaks bread together six times a week. Table time reinforces the gratitude I have for my family.

Research shows that our need to connect with others is just as important as food and water. Eating meals together as a family meets this need and allows each individual to feel a sense of purpose in their life. A strong bond coincides with this self-esteem boost. Self-esteem is a child's best defense against peer pressure.

Below are five suggestions for table time:

Keep it simple. Coming home exhausted from work and immediately making dinner can cause resentment flu. To help prevent resentment flu, I suggest meal planning on a weekly basis and recruiting other family members to help. By delegating a specific task to each family member, you are establishing positive, consistent behaviors. The more everyone contributes the easier it becomes for all involved and good habits are formed.

Prepare for dinner right after breakfast. After we finish breakfast, I chop ingredients and put them in the crock pot. The crock pot is my favorite kitchen utensil! The evenings, my children have practice, we enjoy the simplicity of setting the table and enjoying a hassle free meal.

Playing the game of "Woo Hoo's and Boo Hoo's." During table time our family likes to play a game. We each share a Woo Hoo and a Boo Hoo we experienced during our day. A Woo Hoo is a good experience. A Boo Hoo is an experience we didn't like. These conversations provide problem-solving opportunities. For example, one evening we discovered that my daughter was being bullied at school. The five of us worked together to find a solution and I'm happy to say the two girls are now friends.

Listen to understand. My friend, Dr. Denny Coates, believes "listening is the most powerful skill a parent can possess. It has the potential to "change the game" with regard to your relationship with your child." Our job as parents is to teach the importance of listening by being the example during dinner conversations. Listening to understand opposed to listening to respond is just as important as hugging your child.

Creating the habit of eating together makes holiday gatherings less complicated. As a child, my parents taught me the importance of table time. Today, when my parents, my brother and his family, myself and my family get together during the holidays we truly enjoy each other's company and we openly communicate enabling us to continue to grow our bond. This also allows us to set an example that future generations can follow.

Much like exercise, enjoying dinner together builds muscles of togetherness. I encourage you to maximize your table time.

"Nonverbal communication happens unconsciously and leaves an impression that can last a lifetime. Children thrive when they feel understood."

-Crystal Horton

A COMPLETE LACK OF COMMUNICATION

Our verbal and nonverbal cues can either put our child in defensive mode or provide a calming, effect. According to Steven Handel, a psychology journalist and self-improvement writer, "research suggests that nonverbal communication makes up sixty to seventy percent of all that we communicate." In other words, our actions speak louder than our words.

Let's take a look in the window of a family of four who is preparing for an evening at the recreation center. Mom has had a stressful day at work and is looking forward to a yoga session. Dad has also had a long day at work and is looking forward to taking his frustrations out during a strength training session. Their daughter loves basketball and can't wait for practice. Their son, spending the day at daycare listening to a teething baby, is yearning for affection from his parents.

Prior to going to the gym here's what things looked like. The family arrived home in a rush to eat dinner and get to the gym. Mom is cooking dinner while dad is outside mowing the lawn. Their daughter is searching for her basketball shoes. Their son is whining in the kitchen tugging on mom's leg asking why they have to go to the gym. Mom out of frustration and in a hurry to finish dinner sends her son to his room.

As the family sits around the dinner table, dad is making comments like "hurry up we only have 10 minutes." Their son continues to ask "Why do we have to go?" He gets sent to his room and misses dinner. His question goes unanswered.

Having finally arrived at the recreation center, their daughter immediately rushes off to basketball practice, while mom and dad sign their son into daycare. During the sign-in process their son has a temper tantrum and screams "I don't want to be here, I want to go home!" Because of his tantrum, daycare refuses to watch him.

This unforeseen misfortune leaves mom, dad and their son sitting in the gym waiting for basketball practice to finish. A frustrated mom and dad are left looking at their smart phones unable to unwind from their hectic day. Their son asks if he can have a snack, and a new argument ensues. Mom, staring at her phone responds "I didn't make it to yoga, because of you." Dad, who is also staring at his phone, responds "when we get home you are going straight to bed." Their son, looking at his parents with his head tilted to the side, responds "but I'm hungry." Mom snaps back with "too bad, you should have thought about that before your little tantrum." She never looks up.

As they continue to argue, their son begins to cry and switches from tugging on mom's leg to hugging his dad's arm. Both parents continue to look at their phones as they verbally abuse their son. They are clearly oblivious to what is happening. Their son, once again in trouble, has to sit in the corner for the rest of their daughters practice.
They arrive home and their son goes to bed hungry.

What can we learn about this evening?

During the evening, their son offered several verbal and nonverbal communication cues but because both parents were attempting to avoid the situation, their son went to bed confused, hungry and still yearning for affection. This is an example of parental leadership gone terribly wrong. Our posture imitates our frame of mind. A closed body stance is less inviting to social interaction then an open body stance. Children pick up on this and respond accordingly. In the example above, both parents had a closed body stance, and their son reacted with a whiny, defensive attitude. If the parents had exhibited an open body stance, their son would have responded differently.

The meaning behind body language can be easily recognized if we are paying attention. When their son looked at his parents with a tilted head both parents missed it. The nonverbal gesture both parents presented to their son was that their phones were more important than him. L.R. Knost, a best-selling parenting and children's book author, believes, "the reason teens isolate themselves when they're overwhelmed is because when they're toddlers we [parents] isolate them when they're overwhelmed instead of helping with their problems."

Facial expressions convey the emotions we feel in that moment. Expressions happen quickly and learning to recognize them can reveal what a person is thinking and feeling. Both parents should have observed their son's facial expression which would have helped avoid an unnecessary misunderstandings.

When their son was tugging on his mom's leg and hugging his dad's arm, his nonverbal communication cue was that he craved touch. Individuals crave touch in order to feel secure. A cue the parents missed, was their sons use of tugging in an attempt to get his parents to look him in the eye. Eye contact is a key to determine if a person is actually paying attention.

Both parents spoke to their son in an angry voice which caused him to react in a pleading tone of voice. Verbal abuse comes in many forms including angry outbursts and quiet comments. Nonverbal communication includes behaviors such as our posture, facial expressions, gestures, touch, eye contact and tone of voice. To avoid a situation like this family experienced, parents must learn to communicate effectively through listening ears, watchful eyes and calm tone of voice.

Smart phones have become an avoidance approach to parenting. Thirty minutes per day of uninterrupted, undivided attention with your child fulfills the child's belonging in the family. If you don't have at least thirty minutes to give your child, restructure your schedule. In this example, had both parents given their son thirty minutes they would have picked up on his verbal and nonverbal communication cues and then reacted accordingly.

A good friend of mine, John Page Burton, states, "our body language is often in direct conflict with our verbal communication. Our body language and speech must be in alignment."

Nonverbal communication happens unconsciously and leaves an impression that can last a lifetime. Children thrive when they feel understood.

SPILLED MILK

Have you ever wondered what it's like for a three-year-old child to understand words that come naturally to adults? I believe that a small child has no idea what "adult communication" is. My daughter has said on more than one occasion, "Mom, I don't know what that word means."

For the first few years of life, communication through words is minimal at best. A toddler communicates through actions, facial expressions, and emotions. These skills are a learned behavior based on how we respond to the child's nonverbal communication.

Let me share a personal example. When my children were young, my husband worked out of town four days a week. My youngest was three weeks old, my middle child was one and a half, and my oldest was three. I was exhausted and developed a tired, irritable attitude. My oldest daughter was learning how to talk and enjoyed being my "big helper." One morning, she tried pouring herself a cup of milk and the cup slipped out of her hand, sending milk everywhere.

I became upset with her and failed to recognize that she was taking responsibility by trying to help me. She began to cry uncontrollably. It wasn't until after I cleaned up the mess that I realized the nonverbal message I had given her. My tired, irritable facial expression and my tone of voice sent a message of disapproval for her taking responsibility.

With this realization, I felt horrible for the way I responded to her. I apologized and explained, in a language she could relate to just how much I appreciated her help. The next morning I fixed my mistake by making sure the container had enough milk for her to pour without spilling. I made a huge expression of encouragement and gratitude when she accomplished this.

Children like to help and they enjoy affirmations of love. Viewing the situation from my child's perspective helped me gain clarity on why we had a misunderstanding. Talking with and guiding our children at an early age is crucial. Teaching a child to understand why things are not to be taken personally, provides an opportunity to show why certain situations are just "spilled milk."

Below are some questions we can reflect on when a situation goes terribly wrong:

1. When have you felt that a situation could have turned out differently if you had communicated properly?
2. If you could go back to your childhood what advice would you give yourself?
3. How do you find peace in awkward situations?
4. How does your child find peace?

MAKING SENSE OF A TEMPER TANTRUM

Like all parents, I have my ups and downs. When my four-year-old is screaming and kicking the floor, my gratitude for life can quickly disappear. I believe that anger breathes anger. When my child is screaming, I want to scream too. The question I'm often asked is: "How do we control it?" That is the wrong question to ask!

If we control and place conditions on the tantrum our child is having, why would they stop? Wouldn't that just fuel the fire for them to scream louder and kick the floor harder? How did we feel as child when we were told to stop and be quiet? Didn't you want to do the opposite and take a stand? I know I did!

During my child's temper tantrums, I have learned to pay attention to the words that are being said as well as what is not being said. In the moment, I may not know what to say or how to heal and help, but that's all right. As a parent we are learning at the same time our child is. "Please Stop" is what my four-year-old son yells, when he doesn't get his way. Those two words are my ten-second warning before a temper tantrum emerges. Here's an example of what I discovered during one of our recent misunderstandings.

We were in public at an after school activity. My son and I were getting out of the car to walk across the parking lot and meet my daughters at the other end. On the drive he had fallen asleep and was resting comfortably in his car seat. I woke him up to walk across the parking lot. A ten-minute task turned into a thirty-minute drama scene.

I held my son's hand as I pulled him along. My son began screaming "please stop" as he hit my arm. He was upset that we had to get out of the car because he was tired and wanted to sleep. I knew if I let go of his hand he would plop his little body on the concrete and I would lose what little control I had. Others began to experience his tantrum which made me uncomfortable. I felt like I was being watched, and assumed that I would be judged by how I handled this situation. I kept telling myself "he's tired," after all, we had gone fishing earlier, and he had missed his normal thirty minute nap.

The crowd watched my son continue to yell "please stop, mom" while he hit my arm, I found myself clamping my jaw shut because I wanted to yell "please stop" back. My first instinct was to offer a "people pleasing" excuse. I was embarrassed and extremely frustrated but still wanted to excuse his misbehavior. My ego was in overdrive.

We only had a few more steps to go, and I was trying to remember any tips or tools from a recent parenting class that might help with this situation. Honestly, what I realized was that none of my parenting classes ever covered the hitting and screaming step. I knew by giving in to his behavior, I would be giving him the result he sought. I decided to take matters into my hands right then and there.

I looked my son directly in the eyes and with a stern voice I told him "You will walk with me to get your sisters and if you continue to scream and hit me you will not be included in any activities this evening. What would you like to do?" He realized that he was no longer in control of the situation, he quickly picked choice number one.

My son likes to be in control. When he feels out of control, he tests the waters, which usually comes in the form of a temper tantrum. When I give in, his behavior gets worse. I'm supporting his behavior. This "learned" behavior can easily carry into adulthood if I don't address it now.

Parenting is an ongoing process whereby we learn from each experience. During this particular moment I realized what I teach my children now will carry into adulthood. Sometimes, during a temper tantrum we place judgment on ourselves and wonder what others are thinking of us? When this happens, our subconscious mind is offering up thoughts of judgment. For example, when I was worried about what others were thinking my awareness intensified that thought!

When I take a step back and identify why my child is having a tantrum, I realize he doesn't know how to use his words and this is something I can teach him. Together, a parent and child learn to nurture, love and guide each other. Adapting to a new way of thinking takes time. The key is to be flexible as each day provides a new obstacle to work on in your parent-child relationship.

Will this make the tantrum calmer? No, however, it builds muscles of patience. Patience requires practice. Once I became aware of my surroundings, I learned to create positive action steps before moving forward.

Below are five questions I ask myself that help build my
"muscles of patience."

1. Why is my child upset?
2. What happened prior to the tantrum?
3. How much "undivided attention" have I given my child?
4. When was the last time we did something they wanted to do?
5. How do we move forward?

With three children and a busy schedule, temper tantrums will happen. The more I become aware of the triggers, the more I know my limits. Providing a structured routine, keeping an eye on frustration levels and taking care of myself, help me stay sane.

WHEN PARENTING WENT TERRIBLY WRONG

Recently, I made a huge mistake. My eight-year-old daughter and I had a misunderstanding regarding chores. We began a discussion about why family contributions play an important role in our household. Being the strong willed child she is, she resisted my point of view, and I found myself getting more and more frustrated. Suddenly, I blurted out "You're grounded, go to your room." She gave me a strange look about the same time I was thinking to myself "Why did I just say that?" I realized she had never been grounded. Our misunderstanding went into hyper drive.

In reality, I had sent her to her room so that I could cool off and figure out my next move. Because she was confused, she kept coming out of her room wanting to ask questions. I wanted to think before we talked so I kept sending her back to her room and she kept coming back out and asking more questions. Without thinking, I added 14 more days to her punishment. She didn't have a clue what grounded for one day meant let alone fourteen more? I had effectively backed myself into a corner and had no exit strategy.

That evening my husband and I searched for ways that we

could fix MY MISTAKE and how we could reverse MY misguided "groundation."

We designed a points system that was based on her future actions. For every 100 points she earned she would earn a day back from being grounded. The points system was as follows:

Help prepare Breakfast	50 points
Help prepare Lunch	50 points
Help prepare Dinner	50 points
1 Load of Laundry	100 points
Clean and Organize Garage	50 points
Empty Dishwasher	25 points
Wipe table/sweep floor after each meal	25 points
Wipe table chairs after each meal	25 points
Clean Microwave	25 points
Take out Trash & Re-bag	10 points
Clean Bathroom	100 points
Mop Floors	50 points
Dust	25 points
Write it out:	100 points

The first day we had her write the entire scenario of what happened. How she felt, how others felt and what actions could have changed. SOMEHOW she managed to see something and made a decision within herself to change. I could see her making positive changes. Talk about reverse psychology!

Immediately she began taking care of her morning routine which normally takes an hour "with reminders" yet she finished in thirty minutes. She then tackled the list of things to do and earned back two days in just a couple hours.

The next day, as we were working together in the garage, my daughter apologized for her actions and discussed how embarrassing it would be for her to have to tell her grandmother what happened. I asked why she would be embarrassed, and she openly stated "even though I am embarrassed I must take complete responsibility for my actions." Wow! I was amazed by the lesson I was learning from her that was unfolding over being mistakenly grounded.

Over the next few days, she earned six days back and successfully negotiated with us to attend a barbecue with her friend. When she got home from the barbecue, she figured out how to earn more days back. She experienced a feeling of accomplishment all on her own. Her confidence changed because she knew that she could take on more than she thought.

By virtue of MY mistake my daughter had no choice but to become a more self-reliant child. Would I handle this situation the same way again? No! What I learned from MY MISTAKE was that when I'm frustrated I need to be the one to take a time out.

Rather than sit down and communicate my frustrations with my daughter I proceeded with my mistake and added more confusion to the situation. It would have clearly made more sense for me to take a time out in the heat of the moment and recollect my thoughts before moving forward with any decision.

"The more I researched and studied healthy parenting patterns the more I was able to change."
-Crystal Horton

REFLECT BEFORE YOU RESPOND

The messages we convey to our children today will stay with them for the rest of their lives. Whether the message we share is happy, sad or somewhere in the middle, our message will make an impact. Planting fear based thoughts in children can turn them into fearful adults.

For example, when a parent is asked by their child "What is an alarm system?" The response may come in one of two ways:

1. *"This system is used as a smoke and carbon monoxide detector."* Typically, the child would shrug their shoulders and go back to what they were doing.

2. *"This system will keep you safe when sleeping, because if someone were to break in, the alarm would go off and alert the cops. We wouldn't want anyone kidnapping you while you're asleep."* This response will lead to questions of "What is kidnap?" As the parent digs a deeper hole, the child will start to feel insecure and possibly start fearing for their

life. Fear of the dark or being alone can cause many sleepless nights.

Below are three helpful tips to bring awareness to the importance of effective communication:

Think things through before you respond. Recently my niece asked, "Why are you Hispanic? What does Hispanic mean?" I could have responded in a way that would have introduced her to the history of racism, knowing that a simple response can have a powerful impact.

Respond with care. I proceeded with care in my response to my niece's question. I know that my answer could easily form her opinion of the different cultures in America. Appreciating my cultural background I answered informatively. I was also able to provide her with a plethora of examples from different books, family pictures and recipes.

Take responsibility for future generations. The messages we share with our children may also be the messages shared with future generations. Intentional living produces seeds of positive growth and a thirst for knowledge. The more we can help our children research their own questions and network with others, the better the chances future generations will flourish.

The answers we offer can cause a negative or positive effect on our child's psyche. Clearly understanding our family values helps deepen our connection to our child, especially when asked questions. Remember, our actions speak louder than words but it's our words that create the decision to act.

FIVE-MINUTE HUG

Like most kids, my children engage in a lot of trivial conflicts. For example, they argue about who gets in the car first, who gets out of the car first and who sits next to dad at the dinner table. They argue about being in each other's personal space and whose toys belong where. They seem to argue for the sake of arguing!

Over the years, I've attempted to solve their conflicts with an array of different strategies including letting them figure it out, separating them, time outs, talking it out with them, teaching a lesson through problem-solving and punishment. Nothing worked! One evening two of my children started arguing over who got to brush their teeth first. My husband told them "that's it, you two have to hug for five minutes." After a few seconds of shock they laughed, hugged and then worked out a solution. It was something simple that led to a positive, productive resolution.

My husband and I believe that being actively engaged with our children is what makes our parenting style work. A "five minute" hug allows our parenting style to be consistent without feeling guilty. Ultimately, we are teaching our children how in less than five minutes they can transform an argument into a positive result.

Below is an interview with my children regarding their thoughts on a five-minute hug.

What is a five-minute hug?

Aubrey (7): "Five minutes of hugging the person you are arguing with, and figuring out how to get out of the hug."

Addison (5): "I have to hug my brother because I was mean."

David (4): "uh- it means hug."

Do you like hugging when you're arguing with your sibling?

Aubrey: "No it's upsetting because we don't want to."

Addison: "It's ok."

David: "Yes, because we wrestle when we hug."

How do you feel after a five-minute hug?

Aubrey: "Confused."

Addison: "Good."

David: "Happy."

Do you think a five-minute hug helps you to stop arguing and become buddies again?

Aubrey: "Yes."

Addison: "Yes"

David: "Yes"

Thomas Winterman, a child therapist, school counselor and author, explains "The goal of punishment is not so the child wallows in self-pity, crawling on their hands and knees while begging for forgiveness. Your parental discipline style goes so far beyond what you actually do – such as spanking, timeouts, scolding and restriction. Your parental discipline is a part of your system and cannot be separated from who you are. It's the way you talk, the way you react, the way you treat others and the way you praise your child, etc.."

What works for us may not work for you and your family. Pay attention to your parenting style. If you find yourself frustrated in the middle of your trivial conflicts, recognize that it's time to find a different solution. Seek advice from other parents who have children the same age or Google examples and outcomes. If that doesn't work, hire a family coach. Your children should be learning a lesson in resolving sibling conflict not a temporary lesson on manipulation.

OVER PROTECTION FLU

If I could wrap my children in bubble wrap, I would. Does that make me an overprotective/helicopter parent? Perhaps it does, but only if I actually do it. As a parent, I often find myself becoming the overly protective parent type that shields my children from EVERYTHING. From my perspective, I am protecting them from biohazards, tornados and possibly death. From their perspective, they just want to ride their bike around the neighborhood.

Here's a recent example. We moved from a small town of 5,000 people to a large town of 150,000 people. My "momma bear" radar was on high alert. We moved to a new neighborhood, and I found myself hushing my children for fear of being too loud. We joined a new church, and I found myself constantly hovering over every event. I became overly concerned because everything was different, and I was uncomfortable with the thought of my children being uncomfortable. My "over protection" caused my children to begin acting fearful. They were catching the over protection flu.

When I attended their school orientation, I found myself wanting to pack our bags and go back to our former town.

All I heard and saw were the negatives in our new environment. I didn't see the smiles and excitement on my children's faces as they experienced their new environment. They were more than willing to be uncomfortable; I was the one who was having the hard time.

Helen Williams, a parent counselor and family educator, explains "overprotective parenting gives children the message that they can't be trusted and that they are incapable of normal events that other children handle with ease." What I failed to recognize was that I was pushing my own fears from childhood onto my children. I believed that my children could only function if I made all of their decisions for them. I believed it was my job to convince them that everything was fine. I now recognize there is a fine line between encouraging my children to think on their own and keeping them safe. Rather than continue to teach them to fear their surroundings I encourage them to leave their comfort zone and reach their own conclusions. With that being said, my momma bear" radar is still turned on.

Below are three tips to help ward off over protection flu:

Embrace Change. When experiencing something new, it's normal to feel fearful. My husband says that "the feeling of fear is weakness leaving your body, just keep going and you'll feel better." Failing to teach children what the world is about shields them from experiencing life. Living in fear is no way to live. Embracing change teaches children to adapt to a new environment.

Teach children to step out of their comfort zone. I have learned that becoming comfortable with anything requires that I embrace being uncomfortable. Not everything is a worst case scenario. For example, by encouraging my children to introduce themselves to others and make new friends, I am teaching them to be assertive. Telling children not to talk to strangers is confusing. Isn't everyone a stranger, until you meet them? Teaching children to be aware of possible predators who may want to harm them is teaching them to be discerning.

Allow room for mistakes. We are human and humans make mistakes. Mistakes are part of learning. The magic happens when we learn from our mistakes. Hunter Maats and Katie O'Brien, authors of Straight-A Conspiracy, explain "Telling students they need to take advantage of the feedback they get isn't just good advice – it's established science." They also go on to explain mastering something takes "ten thousand hours of deliberate practice to become an expert in almost any field." Allowing room for mistakes not only encourages failure but continues to provide positive outcomes.

Creating a path toward change allows our children to learn and grow. How can children learn to become unique, extraordinary, silly, responsible, sincere, humble, wise and happy without first having the experience of being uncomfortable?

HELICOPTER VS ENGAGED PARENTING

I'm a recovering "helicopter parent." A helicopter parent is known as an over protective, over controlling and over perfecting parent. I believe the origin of my hovering instincts stems from the traumatic experience of my oldest son's death. I struggled for several years with the fear of losing another child. To calm my fear, my natural reaction was never to miss a thing. I experienced far too many sleepless nights checking in on my children, making sure they were breathing. Thoughts of worry and concern dominated my mind. I honestly thought I was protecting my children. Not once did I recognize the only thing I was doing was reinforcing my own fear.

I raised fearful toddlers who were overly alert to their surroundings. I consistently asked questions like "What are you doing? Where are you going? Why are you doing that?" I didn't let my children breathe freely or learn through their own experiences. I didn't allow them to do anything alone.

When my children slept over at a family member's home, I would call or send text messages, checking in every chance I got. I began to give off the "I don't trust you" vibe. My children didn't go outside without my permission. They couldn't eat without me being present. I made sure we were always together.

In the meantime as my hovering got worse, I lost contact with friends. My health was terrible, I refused to exercise. I stopped scheduling time for myself. I encouraged date nights with my husband at home. I simply stopped living. The more I fueled my controlling patterns, the worse my surroundings became.

I was confused about how to be an involved parent without smothering. Dr. Anne Dunnelwood, Ph.D. a licensed psychologist and author of Even June Cleaver Would Forget the Juice Box, explains "the main problem with helicopter parenting is that it backfires." My results from over parenting were that my children had undeveloped coping skills, increased anxiety, a sense of entitlement and stunted life skills.

Once I became aware of what I was doing, I had to change my behaviors. This was quite the challenge. The more I researched and studied healthy parenting patterns the more I was able to change. As I developed into an engaged parent, my children's feelings of love and acceptance increased. Their self-confidence flourished. Today, my oldest daughter is self-motivated with a 4.O grade point average. My youngest daughter is excelling athletically and academically. My son is a locally recognized artist and is also academically talented. Their social skills are much better because I let go and moved out of their way.

As for me, I have my life back. I'm exercising regularly, socializing and building great friendships as I build my business. I also have time to volunteer and I love it. My husband and I have dates outside our home and we enjoy every second of it. I'm finally free of my demons. I forgave myself and released the fear of unknown from my traumatic experience.

My recommendations for Engaged Parenting vs. Helicopter Parenting

Promote responsibility instead of dependability*. Kids who are dependent on others expect the world to wait on them. As a child grows into an adult this expectation continues. Karen Ruskin, Psy.D., author of The 9 Key Techniques for Raising Respectful Children Who Make Responsible

Choices says "Ingraining responsibility in children is not a trick, but is simply teaching them life skills." Responsibility is a life skill that teaches a child to learn through experience, let them help.

For example teach your child how to make their own bed, rather than doing it for them. Use words of instruction while your child learns how to make their bed. Switch roles and have your child teach you what they have learned. Once a skill is mastered let them do it on their own without nagging or reminding them.

Teach accountability instead of blame. Children tend to devalue themselves when they engage in the blame game. Teaching a child to take responsibility for their actions is emotionally healthy. Self-awareness is focused on a child's ability to judge their own behaviors.

For example, a parent is accountable for guiding a child by acknowledging their actions and decisions. If a child takes a toy from another child teaching them to "say sorry" encourages manners. But, if a parent teaches a child to acknowledge what they did wrong by asking questions that guide the child to recognize an apology is necessary, that teaches accountability. Amy McCready, a parent expert and founder of Positive Parenting Solutions, explains "The fact is that while forcing kids to apologize in the heat of the moment often makes parents feel better, it does little to help children truly understand the effects of their misbehavior."

Teach a child to take pride in making decisions rather than being indecisive. A helicopter parent makes all the decisions and controls the outcome. When the child is away from the parent they tend to become indecisive. "Recurring indecision is a debilitating trait. In the long-term, it can negatively affect well-being, life satisfaction, and success in relationships and work," says Renee Jaine, Chief storyteller at GoZen.com, anxiety relief programs for kids.

A child that takes pride in making decisions forms healthy habits. Encourage your child to make a decision by giving them two options. Start off with simple decisions, "Would you like to make a ham or chicken sandwich for your school lunch today?" Educating your children on the decisions they make is an excellent way to think before they act. At times this may not always be the case, but teaching this life skill to them could decrease the amount of peer pressure they face.

Be the example instead of the moderator. Coaching children through their life experiences is a valuable type of engaged parenting. Asking questions that help guide a child toward taking responsibility for their actions, learning to be accountable and making decisions will help them process disappointment. We can't always be there for our child but we can teach them the life skills to mature through experience.

"Relaxation is an important priority for the spiritual, mental and physical well-being of the family."
-Crystal Horton

THE GREAT TREE HUNT

A holiday tradition is defined as a belief or behavior that is passed down from generation to generation and has a symbolic meaning from the past. Our top priority is to make laughter a tradition during the holidays. The possibilities in our family seem to be endless.

When our family comes together through tradition, we create lasting memories. I believe the main theme in each of our traditions is laughter. After all, laughter relieves tension, stress, elevates the mood, enhances creativity and boosts energy. For example, every year at Thanksgiving we purchase a tree permit, pack up some snacks and make a trip to the mountains in search of the Horton family Christmas tree. This family tradition started when our oldest child was born. Over the years, it has turned into quite the adventure.

The first year we searched for our family tree in a blizzard. When we brought the tree home, it was 6 inches too tall for our vaulted ceilings! That was hilarious!

On another occasion when our oldest child was two-years-old and our youngest had just started crawling, we thought it would be a good idea to take a snowmobile with us. The snowmobile didn't fit the four of us, so my youngest child and I stayed in the truck and waited for our fabulous tree. Forty minutes later, I laughed hysterically as the tree came rolling down the hill, my husband chasing after it and BAM the tree hit the back of our truck.

Last year our kids were old enough to hike into the mountains and search for the Horton family tree. It turned out to be a great deal of fun. We found deer poop which meant "the reindeer must be training for Santa's sleigh" but we didn't find the perfect tree. The kids were thirsty, hungry and tired, so we headed back home. On the way home, my husband, decided to leave us in the truck while he found a tree. A few minutes later he appeared with a 7-foot tree slung over his shoulder. Over the years, our tree hunting adventures have brought us a great deal of laughter.

Traditions can also tell a story about the family. They provide children insight into the family history. This plays an important role in a child's personal identity, strengthens the family bond and teaches values. Continuing family traditions is a great way to connect generations. Positive childhood memories instill a sense of belonging. Memories and family traditions can also create a strong family bond. My husband and I have fond memories of growing up and growing closer thanks to our family traditions. It is important to us that our kids have a similar experience.

THE MAGICAL PAIR OF GLASSES

My oldest daughter is eight. She is becoming quite confident in describing her concerns. Recently I took her to the doctor's office for her annual physical. As a rule, she sits in a chair and stares at the wall but this time it was different. She asked a specific question. "When I wake up in the morning my vision is blurry and sometimes I have trouble seeing the words in my books. What can we do about that?"

It's important to understand that five minutes prior to her asking this question she scored 20/20 vision. As the doctor listened to her concern, he responded "well, maybe your mom can pick up a pair of glasses to help you with that." He looked at me and winked. After my daughter had left the room, the doctor explained to me the positive impact a "magical pair of glasses" can do for a child her age.

That evening I went to the store and searched for a non-prescription pair of glasses. I brought them home and gave them to my daughter. Her face lit up with glee, much like a kid getting a new pair of shoes that they believe makes them run faster and jump higher. Instantly she could see better, and I could tell her confidence was growing because of this "magical pair of glasses."

Over the next few weeks, she began believing words on the page were easier to see. She was reading at a faster pace and comprehending the messages more clearly than ever. She read more books, math made sense, and multiplication became a breeze. Who knew that this "magical pair of glasses" would create a math wizard?

Her classmates responded differently to her and also began treating her as the go-to resource for mind-boggling questions. Prior to her "magical pair of glasses" my daughter hardly spoke in class, she was an observer and saved socializing for home. This "magical pair of glasses" gave my daughter a boost of confidence that allowed her to grow socially, improve her studies and believe in herself. All it took was something as simple as acknowledgment and a "magical pair of glasses."

TELLING THE TRUTH

Recently our oldest daughter asked, "Is Daddy the Easter Bunny?" She had figured it out, thanks to reading the book "Smile," written by Raina Telgemeier. Her reaction was priceless. Her facial expression was like someone walking into a surprise party. She laughed at the thought of how funny it was to think that the Tooth Fairy was real. Throughout the day she chuckled over how her Dad and I knew how to play pretend. I could clearly see this was a tradition she enjoyed. We discussed the symbolic meaning of creativity and imagination.

I'll bet most would say the Easter Bunny played a positive role in their childhood. During my research for this article, I discovered some parent's have concerns about the lie they're telling. There are some that still hold grudges thirty years later. Some have gone to the extreme of no longer believing in God. I was appalled by the arguments that took place in the comment section of certain blog articles.

It is my belief that imaginary cartoons, super hero action figures, barbies and princess' provide a symbolic meaning of hope, allowing us to believe in our dreams and face our biggest fears. Santa Clause, the Easter Bunny, Leprechauns and the Tooth Fairy all provide us with a valuable lesson in the spirit of giving. These traditions are fun and build a foundation of not taking things so seriously. These fantasy characters can help children "cross-over" during a milestone, such as losing a tooth.

Perhaps it's in the way we explain our "lie" to the child when the truth is discovered. A surprise represents the spirit of giving and participating in the joy of "an unexpected event, fact or thing." A secret represents "something meant to be kept hidden or unseen by others." I have effectively communicated to my children that surprises are fun and encouraged but secrets are bad. If anyone tells my child to keep a secret and "not tell anyone" I react negatively. My children understand that this is wrong and they should tell a responsible adult immediately.

The Easter Bunny is a tradition my family chooses to participate in. Therefore, we take the responsibility for preparing our children for this unexpected surprise. Below is a letter I found on Pinterest and recently shared with my daughter. I felt it explained the fun of our surprise and the meaning of why we participate in this tradition.

Dear Aubrey,

When you asked about the Easter bunny, you asked a good question. We know that you want to know the answer, and we had to give careful thought to what to say. The answer is no. We are not the Easter bunny. There is no Easter bunny.

We are the people who fill your basket because we choose to. Just as our parents did for their parents and we did for them.

The Easter bunny is lots of people who keep the spirit alive. He lives in our hearts. The Easter bunny is the magic, love and spirit of giving to others. What he does teach children is to believe something they can't see or touch. Throughout your life, you will need this capacity to believe in yourself, your family, you friends and in God.

Love,
Mom, and Dad

BORING DAYS

Relaxation is an important priority for the spiritual, mental and physical well-being of the family. There are numerous opportunities to keep our kids "entertained," however is entertainment the message we want them to internalize? Providing our children with balance and teaching them how to prioritize health, spiritual and mental happiness creates a productive environment.

Recently my family experienced an over scheduling dilemma. I dreaded hearing the question "What are we doing tomorrow?" There is always something to do, someplace to be and some event to attend. After reciting our agenda, my kids go to sleep happy, knowing there is an adventure the next day. On the other hand, I go to sleep exhausted, thinking about the next day's activities.

On the rare evenings when we have nothing planned for the next day, my kids go to bed upset and refuse to fall asleep. My daughter, Addison recently shared her disappointment by saying: "So, that's it then, tomorrow will be boring?" Ironically these are the nights I get my best sleep!

Our "boring days" consist of sleeping in, watching cartoons, playing with toys, cooking breakfast together and sometimes we just stare at the wall in silence. I feel as if we are taking in each moment, as slowly as we can. Our best talks happen on "boring mornings."

During our "boring afternoons," we have plenty of time for creativity. Once we discovered a nature trail in our backyard and created "nature bags." The kids searched for interesting leaves, rolly pollies, worms, rocks and dinosaur bones. My son discovered and declared "rolly pollies don't eat or poop because they don't have butts or heads." Silly, memorable moments seem to happen when we stay home.

I love our boring moments and find myself yearning for more. Mimi Doe, the author of Busy but Balanced: Practical and Inspirational Ways To Create a Calmer, Closer Family, encourages parents to "Give themselves permission to step off the fast track, trusting that you're giving [your children] the best gift: being present in their lives without being exhausted."

"Organized activities can help children gain skills and self-confidence, but too much structured activity can contribute to anxiety, stress, and depression and cause them to become self-critical perfectionists," as reported in a 2006 study by the American Academy of Pediatrics. I had taught my children that our home was boring, and the only way to stay entertained was to engage in an activity. I realize the events we choose to participate in are decisions we make. I can alter our schedule with additional "boring days" and weekends while also teaching my children the importance of being home and being present.

"This monumental moment would shape her opinion of death for the rest of her life."
Crystal Horton

WHY CAN'T GRANDMA BE LIKE JESUS?

As we finished up our normal bedtime routine, I leaned over to kiss my daughter goodnight. Suddenly, Addison, burst into tears and said: "Why can't (great) Grandma be like Jesus?" I asked her what she meant, and she replied: "I want Grandma to come down from heaven as Jesus did, so she can give me a big hug. I miss her so much." At first I wanted to answer simply, it's just the way it is, part of life, but I didn't because I knew her question deserved a deeper answer than I was prepared to give. I knew the answer had the potential to shape her opinion of death for the rest of her life. I suggested that we set up a meeting with the priest at our church, so he could help answer her question.

When we arrived at the parish office, we were greeted and our conversation began. Addison sat down, crossed her legs, put her right elbow on her knee placed her chin into the palm of her hand looked at the priest and said "Is Grandma having fun in heaven?" As the priest answered her questions, she quickly asked another one. "Is Grandma ok? What is she doing? How do I send her a letter with the picture I drew? Is Grandma a saint? " As the conversation progressed I could see that Addison was beginning to understand that Grandma was ok.

Our meeting also provided a great deal of clarity for me. Today, I view death as a miracle we can't physically see. There are miracles in life that God performs without explanation because the beauty is found in the unknown. When death arrives it is unexpected and unexplained. "Why can't Grandma come down from heaven like Jesus," was a great question. Maybe she does, and we don't see her or maybe she doesn't. None of us know.

This special conversation with our priest was very meaningful. My daughter experienced a spiritual breakthrough and now understands that through prayer "we send letters to heaven." She celebrates when someone dies by baking a cake and sharing stories and memories. She proudly does this because as she says "today they became a saint. That's a big deal, mom." She believes when she draws a picture and tapes it to the wall that "Grandma will see this when I am sleeping."

My daughter once said, "Everything I like is love, and when you don't love anymore, it goes away." The legacy we are building in our home is a foundation that prepares our children for understanding miracles.

SOMETHING'S WRONG

Suicide is something that confuses me. It's not my place to judge what is going through a person's mind when this tragedy happens as I simply don't know. I can recall the terrible thoughts that took over my mind when I was told I had symptoms of depression.

It started out with these crazy cravings for pasta. Then it was sugar cravings, I couldn't get enough pop and candy. Then it was bread. I gained weight rapidly, and I was angry. I began to wonder if I was pregnant; the test came back negative.

When I weighed myself and realized how much weight I had gained I was furious, but I couldn't seem to release the chip bag. I began battling the thoughts in my mind. One thought would be "go for a run, you'll feel better." The other thought would strike back "yum, yum, yum, keep eating."

I would roll my eyes and sigh if my kids asked for any help. I became bitter towards my husband and was infected with the resentment flu. I avoided him as much as possible. After the kids fell asleep, I would lay on the floor because it hurt to do anything more than cry. I cried for hours until my eyes couldn't take anymore, and then I would fall asleep. Eventually, my thoughts attacked my self-confidence. I began to believe I wasn't enough.

I remember putting my hands on my head and shaking it from left to right hoping my thoughts would fall out of my ears. Nothing changed for weeks. During the day I would put my happy face on and at night the voices would return to visit me.

One evening, I locked myself in the bathroom and prayed for help. I commanded that God make my situation change. I spewed words of anger and hatred, demanding that my life be put back together. That night was one of the worst nights of my life!

I pondered becoming a cutter, believing that an open wound could let out all the bad thoughts. Thankfully, this thought didn't become my reality.

I knew I needed help, but I didn't know how to ask for it. I prayed and thankfully my prayers were answered. I talked to my husband and told him that I needed to get help.

We found help, and my road to recovery began. Today, I am healed and no longer have these thoughts. Depression doesn't have to be a silent battle. If you can relate to my experience, I encourage you to seek help.

TAKING A BREAK

Recently, my family went through a major schedule shift. My husband went from working out of town four days a week to working out of state for six weeks. I became the primary, full-time caregiver to our three children.

While my husband was out of town, our son David had a severe asthma attack which sent him to the emergency room. We stayed at the hospital for three days. Fear took over my mind. My parents live in a different city, what do I do with the girls? How do I get them to school? What am I going to feed them? We are out of groceries! The list grew with things I didn't get finished. I worried "now what?" Thankfully, several close friends offered to help. My parents also came to help out. During this time, my husband, who was twenty-one hours away, was completely frustrated.

Once back home, a new experience shook our house. My son had to be hooked up to an oxygen tank which limited his ability to travel to our living room and kitchen. Every four hours an albuterol treatment had to be administered. I was in survival mode, my daughters were taking care of each other while my son was healing.

A few weeks' later things had calmed down, and our family was well on its way back to a semi-normal routine. With my son no longer needing oxygen and my daughters appreciating and understanding the importance of sticking together as a team, we experienced a newfound respect for one another.

At one point, our family was searching for a way to re-charge, re-focus and re-balance after all the events that had taken place in our home. Luckily, my Dad was planning a trip to visit family in Arizona and he invited my oldest daughter and I to go with him.

My husband took time off from work while my daughter and I traveled to Arizona. The drive took 12 hours. I was looking forward to doing absolutely nothing. Aubrey and my Dad shared knock, knock jokes and laughed all the way to Arizona while I took naps. When we arrived, we ate dinner, visited with family and went to bed. I slept 20 hours which allowed my body, mind and spirit to rejuvenate.

The following day we soaked in the sun at a local car show. Aubrey shared stories of things happening at her school and with her friends. We re-connected during our trip and truly enjoyed each other's company. Over the next couple of days, we enjoyed each other's undivided attention. We laughed, colored, played Barbies, put together puzzles and talked about what makes us happy. I discovered how amazing my daughter is at defining what she likes and what she don't like. I learned new things about my daughter I wouldn't have known if we had not taken this vacation.

While we were enjoying our special time together, my husband, Addison and David were experiencing the same type of connection. They learned to move away from the feelings of jealousy because Aubrey had gone with me, they built forts, went swimming, rode bikes and created a recipe for banana nachos.

My husband prepared them for school and handled our drop-off/pick-up routine. He found himself taking naps while they were at school and he learned the importance of a quick re-charge. He became quite creative in encouraging our kids to help out with chores in the evening.

After arriving back home, we shared stories of our experiences. I couldn't help but feel gratitude for the break we took. My husband and I developed a greater appreciation for what it feels like to switch parenting roles.

Often, we get so caught up in our day to day tasks that we fail to recognize how a break can help the entire family re-energize, re-focus, and re-balance. When was the last time you took a break?

20 QUESTIONS

When our children do something for the first time, how do we react? We probably smile, clap and encourage them? Why do we stop? At what point do we go into management mode? "Do this, do that, don't forget to (fill in the blank)...." What's the difference between a newborn and a five-year-old? How did we react when we saw our child experiencing something new? Did we acknowledge and experience it with them or did we miss the moment because we became preoccupied with something else?

How many times a day, do we check our social media sites? How long do we stay on these sites? Do we play with our kids as much as we check our Facebook page? How long do we play with them? How many times do we post pictures of our children just to garner a few likes? Do we even remember the symbolism of the moment we posted on Facebook?

Do we stop working and turn off our electronic devices in order to enjoy the silence of life? Do we turn off our children's electronic devices and encourage outdoor adventures? How much time do we spend sending text messages or checking our email? Do we search for DIY projects and craft ideas that allow us to create special moments with our children?

How many times do our children ask "will you play with me?" How many times do we say "Yes?" How many times do we respond "Not right now, I have a lot to do?" We often wonder why our kids have so much energy and we don't. How much time do we spend with our children each day? If the answer is "not enough" then why not? Ask yourself, what's getting in the way?

How many times do we find ourselves being the one doing the dishes, laundry, mopping, dusting, and vacuuming? Do we start something we don't get around to finishing? Are we burned out? Are we continuously tired? Who can we ask for help? Who wants to help? Are we prioritizing the wrong things? What can we delegate?

To experience a special moment we must to be present. Create the habit of recognizing what you do throughout the day. Be aware of the sounds, the feelings, the taste and the touch of what is around you.

Why do we experience memory loss, lack of spontaneity, irritability or always being late? Could it be that we are not present? When we are present, we are open to being playful. "Being a parent is not about what you give up to have a child but what you've gained from having one" How would you feel if you were more present in every aspect of your life? My guess is that you wouldn't miss as many special moments.

Below are three tips to be present with your child:

Slow down- Join the fun and unwind. A family that plays together stays together. Create memories, be silly and do something fun.

Simplify- Learn to say no. Cut back on activities. This allows your mind time to be more present.

Make eye contact- Most children are emotionally sensitive. Eye contact nourishes a child with love and produces a feeling of mutual respect and trust.

"Our child is an extension of our personality."
-Crystal Horton

SENSE OF BELONGING

I recently participated in a parenting class and the host, Amy McCready, founder of Positive Parenting Solutions, described the importance of a child's need for a sense of belonging to gain a sense of significance in the family. I couldn't help but wonder, isn't this what mothers search for too?

Before a woman becomes a mother, they tend to have a reasonable sense of belonging and they readily identify with the different groups they partake in. Becoming a mother brings up fear of the unknown. A new mom wants to be able to provide and care for her child thus her research on how to do this begins. As a new mother gathers information from books, seminars and the internet, she may become overwhelmed and shocked by this awesome responsibility.

When in doubt, a mom may turn away from this information to avoid feelings of inadequacy they experienced during the research process. A search for significance and belonging usually begins in order to determine where she believes she stands in the family.

The game of "twenty questions" may arise. Will I have a life outside the home? When will I sleep? What if I do something wrong? How will I recover? How will my kids recover? As the questions continue to flow, there are two things moms do. First, avoid change and live in shame and guilt. Or, accept change, study themselves and learn to parent from their strengths. Taking responsibility allows us to build a plan and master balance.

Below are some helpful tips for a balanced environment:

Love you for who you are, today. Two friends shared similar interests. One mom began to compare herself to another mom: "She is thin, has flawless skin and beautiful hair. I don't." In fact, they were both beautiful. A few months later it was discovered the mom she compared herself to was experiencing a disease stemming from taking diet pills.

Don't compare yourself to anyone. Run your race. Focus on yourself, your family, and your values.

Affirm Daily: I am generous, hopeful, confident, joyful, creative, honest, forgiving, compassionate, adventurous, spunky, peaceful, grateful; fearless and delightfully me!

Forgive yourself. You did the best you could with the insight you had at the time. Today, you can accept your feelings of being ashamed for past mistakes because you have learned a better way to handle the situation. It's called learning through experience. Make peace with it and move forward.

Define who you are. When you clearly define and love who you are, your confidence naturally blossoms. Having a positive self-image is important.

- What are three things you like about your physical appearance?
- What are three things you like about your emotional self?

If you have problems answering either of these self-image questions, you may want to seek a life coach to gain some additional awareness.

WHICH MOM ARE YOU?

Every mom has a different parenting style. Our child tends to be an extension of our personality. Many times, moms are the primary caregiver. Read below, which mom style can you relate to?

Creative Mom: Creative mom and her little artists are sitting at the table, eating breakfast and finishing their next artistic piece. Suddenly, her phone alarm goes off and she realizes they only have thirty minutes until school starts. Their mad dash begins.

Creative Mom tells her artists "get your engines ready, whoever finishes first gets chocolate." The tires start smoking, children are flying in every direction and the race is on! Aubrey uses a glittery checklist to mark her progress. Addison and David begin an argument because David wants to wear Addison's rain boots.

The argument continues, there's a loud thud, then it's silent and the screaming begins. The kids start throwing toys at one another. All this is happening while creative mom is squeezing herself into a pair of jeans, a t-shirt and searching for her hat.

Hearing the argument, she runs downstairs "Hey what's going on, it's time to go." As she looks up at her daughter's red t-shirt, she gets the idea to add sparkles to Aubrey's shirt, braid Addison's hair, and make a backpack for David's bear. The kids are happy, all is calm again. In the middle of their projects, Mom realizes they are late for school and out the door they go.

Momma Bear: Her protective instincts flare as little Timmy gets the courage to jump from couch to couch…"No, no, no," she says, "let's not do that, I wouldn't want you to break your arm. How about watching cartoons while I make snacks and then we will go for a walk. You can sit in the stroller."

When snack time is over little Timmy grabs his plate and heads for the sink as Momma Bear says "No, no, no leave it on the table, I'll get it. I wouldn't want you to hurt your toes." When it's time for a walk, Momma Bear straps him in the stroller, then heads to the bathroom. Little Timmy briefly stares at the wall and then they go for their afternoon walk.

Teaching Mom: Suzie asks "hey mom, how do I make a bird house?" Teaching mom gets an idea and she tells Suzie "Grab your jacket we're going for a walk."

During their walk, teaching mom encourages Suzie to look for twigs, leaves, rocks as ways to create her own ideas. As Suzie puts her treasures on the table, teaching mom explains which twig came from which tree and why it's so important to have trees in our world. As teaching mom patiently teaches her daughter how to make a birdhouse out of the materials she has collected, Suzie shows a sense of pride in what she has built.

General Mom: General Mom marches her children from station to station. "Bathroom, kitchen, mud room." When it's time to leave for school the children secure their backpacks, head out the door in a single file line and into the back of the minivan where each child takes their assigned seat and securely fastens their seat belt.

One can't help but wonder if and when these children will ever be allowed the freedom to step outside of "the general's insatiable regimentation" and claim their right to childhood?

Chaotic Mom: As little Johnny's feet dangle through the door of the Maytag front loader, Cindy tries with all her might to turn on the spin cycle knob. Oblivious to it all, "chaotic mom" is putting the finishing touches of lunch for her three children (or is it four, she can't seem to remember).

Chaotic mom balances the phone against her ear as she counsels her best friend Julie on the pro's and con of moving to Ohio. In just a matter of minutes and God willing, chaotic mom will load her "tribe" into the car and make the daily commute to school. During the drive, she will apply her eye shadow using the rear view mirror.

Ultimately, our parenting style is an extension of who we are. One shouldn't take this responsibility lightly. By paying attention to our surroundings and familiarizing ourselves with which mom type we are, we will have a greater impact on our children. You will more than likely identify with a couple of these mom types, but one should be predominant.

BE AN EAGLE

I once read a story about a chicken and an eagle. It was from Darren Hardy's book "Living Your Best Year Ever."

The story starts off on a large, majestic mountainside where a fragile eagle's nest rested. The eagle's nest contained four large eagle eggs. One day an earthquake rocked the mountain causing one of the eggs to tumble down the mountain to a chicken farm, located in the valley below. From instinct, the chickens knew they must protect and care for the egg, so an old hen volunteered to nurture the large egg.

One day, the egg hatched, and a beautiful eagle was born. But the eagle was raised to be a chicken. Soon, the eagle believed he was nothing more than a chicken. The eagle loved his home and family, but his spirit cried out for more. While playing a game on the farm with some of his chicken friends one day, the eagle looked to the skies above and noticed a group of mighty eagles soaring in the skies. "Oh," the eagle cried, "I wish I could soar like those birds." The chickens roared with laughter, "You cannot soar with those birds. You are a chicken and chickens do not soar."

The eagle continued staring, at his real family up above, dreaming that he could be with them. Each time the eagle would let his dreams be known, the other chickens said it couldn't be done. Overtime, the Eagle stopped dreaming and continued to live his life as a chicken. Finally, after a long life as a chicken, the eagle died-a chicken.

What's the moral of the story? If you listen to the chickens around you, you'll live and die like them-a chicken. Deep inside you are an Eagle. Here is your call to soar. You are an eagle. It's time to follow your dreams and not the words of chickens.

Do you desire to live a life of purpose?

I've been working with a client who forgot who she was on the journey to becoming a mom. She felt as if being a mom meant letting go of who she was and she became an angry giver. Her definition of being a mom meant having a clean house, laundry caught up, planning and cooking all the meals, grocery shopping and taking care of the kids. Not once did she mention teaching her children how to live and love life. All she talked about were chores, boring house chores. All work and no play makes for a boring, unhappy

Mom.

Being a Mom is not about chores and not about believing you are a chicken when the mirror clearly shows an eagle. Being a mom is about being a role model and teaching your children about life. You must give yourself permission to move forward. Don't stop being an eagle because you see yourself as a mom.

We all have to fail to achieve success. Being a Mom is GREAT! Letting yourself forget your desires is not being a true mom to your children. You have a child who loves you and cheers for you every step of the way. It's your turn to step up and show your child how precious life is. Go and do what you believe in, teach what you believe and show how amazing it is to live life as an EAGLE!

SHAPING THE FUTURE

Once upon a time there were three moms standing together talking. A person approached them and asked what they did for a living. They each had a different answer. The first mom said, "I'm just a mom." The second mom said "I take care of my children, and keep our house organized." The third mom said," I'm shaping the future."

Moms wear many different hats. Life is full of wonderful treasures. We embrace our role with care and commitment. When a question arises and we are unsure how to answer, we have an extensive network to call and ask for help. We are problem solvers, quick on our feet and ready to serve at any given moment.

Let me share a story with you about a young woman who moved to the United States, from India. She came here eager, a little scared but anxious to meet her husband and start a new life. She was filled with joy and anticipation for the arranged marriage her parents had set up for her. Over the years she learned to cook, clean and carry out every order her husband and in-laws demanded. She became a housemaid. Throughout the years she began to realize her independence was disappearing. When she stood tall to fight for her freedom not only was she mentally and physically abused by her husband but also by her father-in-law. She remained determined to make a change.

Today, she has full custody of her child. They live several states away from her ex-husband and ex-in-laws. She owns a successful business and lives in gratitude. Her values are being restored and she is building a better future for her child.

This story is inspiring to me because although she faced many obstacles, her determination to make a change has shaped a bright future for her child.

We have the choice to be who we desire to be. When given the gift of children, we are given the opportunity to shape the future. We have a voice to contribute and values to share. Give yourself permission to share your pride when you are asked what you do for a living. Being a stay at home mom is an opportunity of a lifetime. Indulge in every second of this blessing.

Sometimes we get caught up in our day to day activities

and fail to celebrate our accomplishments. We tend to focus on what we are doing wrong rather than celebrating what we are doing right. We can be hard on ourselves. We do so much yet give ourselves very little credit. To recognize your accomplishments start with the basics. Celebrate how you manage your household.

Here are a few examples of what moms do:

- Manage schedules and logistics for the entire family.
- Balance priorities to create and manage the budget.
- Motivate, coach and counsel their children.
- Teach and model ethics.
- Work with teachers to monitor academic performance.
- Plan, organize and supervise extracurricular activities.
- Purchase clothing, food and supplies, often under tight budget constraints.
- Prepare and serve nutritious meals to our immediate and extended families.
- Coordinate medical care.
- Drive children to school, team sports, music lessons

and more.

- Negotiate with suppliers, pay invoices, and reconcile accounts.
- Arrange for home and vehicle maintenance and repairs.
- Maintain a clean, organized home.
- Provide hugs, laughter, joy and love.

Hats off to all the Moms out there! Be proud of who you are and who you have become. Being a Mom is a wonderful gift. Remember, our children don't arrive with an instruction manual.

"The way we carry ourselves is what our children may observe and mimic"
-Crystal Horton

MAKING A CHANGE

Tired of picking up, cleaning and cooking on my own, I decided to go on strike! I was tired of begging, pleading and bribing my family to help out around the house. I was simply fed up! My days of exhaustion were over! I was excited at the thought of being able to read my favorite magazine, watch something on television and have more time to write.

Day 1: The house is a disaster. Dishes on the counter, toothpaste in the sink, toys everywhere, clothes on the floor and my husband and kids are getting attitudes. The chaos is taking over my brain, and my need to pick everything up is crawling under my skin. I hope we don't get any unexpected visitors.

Day 2: I begin picking everything up while the kids are at school and then realize "What am I doing? Yesterday will be a wasted day if I pick up." So, I put the mess back and smile.

Day 3: Cleared off my treadmill and began a "run challenge" on Facebook, tagging my running friends to join me in this challenge. What a great way to log some miles and relieve some stress.

Day 4: I will set the example and clean my room and they will do the same. That didn't work!

Day 5: I'm grumpy and very frustrated with the results of my strike! I'm ready to march this family right back into shape. It's time to get this house cleaned! I keep finding myself praying for patience throughout the day.

Day 6: Did I mention that my husband likes order and neatness too? He and the kids had a family meeting, and now the house is SPOTLESS! I can hear the choir singing "Hallelujah" and I can't help but take pride in the fact that I did not budge or volunteer to help!

Day 7: I realized I was the problem!

You see, the family became conditioned to my being in charge of everything. I taught them exactly how to treat me. I taught them that the only way things get done around the house is if I initiate them.

By going on strike and forcing myself to sit through the

storm, my family realized they were more than capable of taking care of the household without mom telling them what to do.

I'M FAT

There once was a group of girls who decided to play "Mom's and Daughters." One girl dressed up as the mother and the other as her daughter. The scene begins in a bathroom where the girls play dress up and put lipstick on. As they compliment each other on their beautiful style, the Mother turns to the mirror gives herself a glance and says "I am so fat!" The other girls laugh and they decide to play something else.

Our children can develop a poor body image because a mother is obsessed with being fat. For example, I know a woman who is 5'10, 150 pounds and takes diet pills. Her daughter is also obsessed with her weight. Having a negative body image can create feelings of shame, embarrassment and anxiety brought forth when we talk about our bodies. People with a negative body image tend to feel their shape or size is a sign of personal failure. Poor body image can cause mental instability, low self-esteem, depression, anxiety, dieting and eating disorders.

A friend of mine encourages a positive body image by keeping a top ten list of things she likes about herself. Her daughter also keeps a top ten list. A positive body image occurs once we have a realistic perception of our bodies, AND we appreciate our bodies as they are. A positive body image involves understanding that attractive, healthy bodies come in many shapes and sizes and that physical appearance says very little about our character or value as a person. A healthy body image means that our assessment of our body is kept separate from our sense of self-worth and ensures that we don't spend an unreasonable amount of time worrying about food, weight, and calories.

Our body image is our belief about our body. It's how we see ourselves, how we think and feel about the way we look and how we think others view us. Our body image can be influenced by those in society, the media, and peer groups. The way we carry ourselves is what our children will observe and mimic. A positive self-image means that we are creating an example for our children to learn from.

MAKE THE DECISION TO INSPIRE

Have you ever put a workout schedule together only to realize it doesn't fit into your family life balance? Have you found yourself hoping to make the routine work but end up becoming frustrated? How about making an effort to get up an hour earlier to get a good workout in? How about staying up late to get some cardio done? Or what about sneaking in a workout during lunch hour?

When I was going through my childbearing years, I gained a lot of weight, and my self-esteem took a hit. I didn't want to be in pictures because I didn't like the way my body looked. It wasn't until much later, that I could acknowledge my body had created beautiful, healthy babies. We all have a choice to sculpt our bodies in the way that we desire them to look. It's my choice. Changing my mindset helped me make the decision to become a role model for my children.

Yes, our schedule, doesn't always work out the way we anticipate. Why is that? We are Moms. We eat problems for breakfast and render solutions and suggestions as we go. Moms create daily routines to get everything done during the day. Introducing something new such as a weekly workout routine may cause everything to feel crammed together.

*Here are some simple suggestions for adding a new goal
into the daily mom routine:*

Make a Decision: Acknowledge this is a lifestyle change
you are making. Rushing through things is not the way to
create consistency. Start by looking at your current
schedule and examine what you can take out or cut back on
that will allow you to incorporate your new goal into your
schedule. Commit to this goal for one month. The next
month include a little more into your routine. Continue
setting consistent goals until you reach your satisfied,
healthy limit. Slow and steady keeps the goal alive. Fast
and crazy causes burn out.

Define Why: Once you have figured out how to make this
goal fit into your Mom routine, define WHY you want to
accomplish this goal. Perhaps you want more energy or
desire to fit into your new jeans, socialize with friends or
just have "me" time to release some stress. Once you define
WHY this is important, be sure to share your goals with
others. Post them on your fridge, social media streams,
the washer and dryer, mirrors or even the ceiling above

your bed. As you continuously remind yourself why, you will become even more motivated to reach your goal. You are also creating a team of accountability partners.

__You're a Role Model__. When you create a change in your life and share your why with others, you have the potential to inspire people with every move you make. Your children watch and learn from you. They learn through the actions you are taking. With every move you make and with every obstacle you tackle your confidence increases. As your children witness your transformation, they will become inspired.

Strive for lifestyle changes that create a positive, uplifting, confident difference for you and your family. What action steps can you create today that will inspire you as well as others to follow you on your journey?

STOP WAITING FOR PERMISSION

I feel guilty when I'm away from my family. I have felt guilty for taking a slow shower or giving myself an hour to get ready. For me, guilt has become the "white elephant" in the room. In my subconscious, I created some unrealistic expectations of what motherhood is. As a child when I fell and got hurt I usually blamed someone else and then held a grudge. I believed it wasn't my responsibility and that someone else should have been watching me.

Now, as a parent and because of the grudges I held as a child, I find myself a guilt filled mother who can't seem to take a shower in peace. I feel like it's my responsibility to be the buffer for every adversity my children face. For example, last week my daughter fell at school, and I got upset because I wasn't there to help her. In reality, I couldn't and realized I must let go.

I recognize that most of my guilt programs can be traced back to childhood grudges. I must learn to accept and move away from the past. I must also accept that my children will experience pain. This thought is a challenge for me. I'm slowly learning to let go of my fear and allow my children to learn for themselves.

In my quest for a successful career, great health, financial well-being and a happy life, I often find myself on the short end. I feel like I'm waiting for a "magic bullet" to pop out of nowhere and propel me toward a guilt-free, limitless life. I'll just wait for the "magic bullet."

As I write this, I'm finding myself feeling guilty for not smothering my children with love and attention. Has guilt become an avoidance strategy? Is it rational to think that my children need me to such a degree that I cannot take a shower, workout, build my business or participate in other worldly pleasures? Certainly I shouldn't have to wait until they graduate?

I recently made the decision to focus on what is causing me to feel guilty, and I realize I must stop waiting for permission. Guilt has become my avoidance strategy. I'm aware that my feeling of guilt may still be a distraction as I work my way toward my goals and dreams. I will address it when it comes up.

At times, I realize I wait for permission to live my life and with this awareness comes a sense of relief. I have begun giving myself permission to be happy. I'm surprised by the blessings that lie on the other side of guilt.

"Our curiosity should replace our fear of the unknown and awaken our sense of wonder."

-Crystal Horton

DEVELOPING A MOMPRENEUR MINDSET

In the world of a "MomPreneur," our mindset is our most valuable asset. Keeping our mind clear and focused brings clarity to both our business and family life.

I recently watched an interview with Success Magazine founder Darren Hardy, where he shared a quote that made a profound impact on me. "Your mind is like a clean glass of water. As the negative thoughts of doom and gloom form in your mind, that clear glass of water becomes dirty. By feeding that thought, your mind will continue to create a dirty glass of water. If you place the dirty glass of water under the faucet, it will flush out the dirty water, leaving a glass full of abundant minded thoughts. It is critical to flush our glass continuously." Being creative, balanced and curious helps a person flush their glass.

Working and raising children can cause us to become creative. I find that when the kids aren't happy, I'm usually in a flustered state of mind. What's a creative alternative? I like to pack up the swim bag and drive to the "rec center". The kids are happy and entertained in the pool and I can get in a couple hours of work. Win, win. Remember, in today's world your office can be anywhere. Creativity equates to a happy family, happy mom and happy mind.

When I hear of the word balance, I think of a yoga instructor sitting in a rainforest, eyes closed, breathing deep breaths with no interruptions. As a MomPreneur, this fantasy is far from my reality. I know when it's quiet; the kids are usually up to no good. To a MomPreneur, a peaceful, balanced mindset, to a MomPreneur, is children giggling, playing and running around creating their brilliant mosaic. The key to attaining balance lies in our ability to make decisions. First we must define what the word balance means to us. For me, creating and maintaining balance means being prepared and staying connected to my environment.

Our curiosity should replace our fear of the unknown and awaken our sense of wonder. Simply put, curiosity creates momentum and a happy, positive mindset. As a MomPreneur, I am constantly discovering new, creative, time-saving tips to implement as I awaken new opportunities. While this is happening our family bond becomes clear and amazingly fun because things are getting done efficiently. Momentum is happening!

According to Charles Haanel, author of the Master Key System,"You cannot entertain weak, harmful, negative thoughts ten hours a day and expect to bring about beautiful, strong and harmonious conditions by ten minutes of strong positive, creative thought."

Here are a few tips. When curling your eyelashes in the morning come up with a solid affirmation to recite instead of counting to thirty. As you get ready for the day instead of listening to music or watching the news, search for a podcast or YouTube channel featuring motherhood, parenting, time management tips, entrepreneurship or positive thinking.

Small, simple changes create a peaceful, positive mindset full of curiosity and momentum.

BUSINESS FROM HOME

Have you ever found yourself bribing your kids so you can get through a phone conversation without being interrupted? Below are five tips to help minimize interruptions whenever they show up.

Create a Habit: Whenever possible schedule your calls in advance, preferably when your kids are at school, etc. Scheduling in advance gives you time to prepare and pay respect to the person you are speaking with. Consider the fact it takes 30 days to create a new habit. You will also be teaching a new routine to other family members and allowing them time to understand how they are playing a significant role in contributing to the "family business."

Be Prepared: When possible, study and prepare for your phone call. You will also want to prepare things for the kids to do while you are on the phone. Preparation can remove the frantic panic before a call and eliminate any possible interruptions that may take place while you're on the phone.

15 Minute Rule: Interact with your children 15 minutes prior to a scheduled phone call. Give them your undivided attention and be willing to play whatever activity they choose. When the 15 minutes is over, explain to them how much you have enjoyed that special time and that you are looking forward to playing more after you finish your phone call.

Communicate: Explain the importance of the call. Create clarity of what the ultimate goal is. Creating an end goal with your children helps explain what you are doing. When you leave the door closed to talk on the phone or get other work done, referring to the goal will help the child understand. Once you have their buy in it will cut your interruption rate by 50%.

Design a family vision board: For example, when cutting out pictures of Disneyland explain, "this is why I make phone calls, so that we can enjoy this experience together." When it's time to make calls you can refer to the family vision board. A family vision board helps create an end vision for the family to celebrate when the goal is reached. Make sure to enjoy some high fives along the way. After the phone call celebrate how you worked together as a team.

With a little preparation and a lot of love, you and your children can enjoy creating a business together. By taking ownership of your schedule and implementing time management strategies you and your children can work as a team to reach your business goals.

CREATE A FAMILY VISION BOARD

How do you describe your goals to your family? Creating a family vision board that highlights your goals can bring clarity to the entire family. A family vision board can also serve as a guide to refer to when family members have questions about why you are on the phone, going to meetings or engaged in other business related functions.

Materials:

1. Commitment aka Glue
2. Determination aka Scissors
3. Pride and Passion aka Poster Board
4. Vision aka Pictures, phrases, words, photos of self and family

Find a high profile location for your vision board: Start with your family mission statement then collect and affix pictures that correspond to your goals.

Seek Balance: Include pictures of things that would be amazing to experience both as a family and individually. Include goals that define commitment, determination, pride, and passion.

Creating balance is the key. For example, A person cannot go on a vacation with the family if their health and finances are not in place.

Family Contributions: Creating a family vision board shows each family member how they can play a significant role in your business. They also contribute to the success of the business because each of them is doing their part. Contributions can include picking up around the house, drying the dishes, sweeping and cleaning.

When everyone is working toward the same goal, the journey becomes much more productive and enjoyable.

LIFE LESSONS FROM A LEMONADE STAND

A Lemonade Stand is an activity that children enjoy doing and they can earn money to purchase things they like. Children invite the neighborhood to enjoy in this adventure with them. Their excitement can also impact adults who have fond memories from childhood.

In my research, I have found little information on how parents can teach their children about entrepreneurship. I have chosen the Lemonade Stand. Teaching my children how to own and operate their very own lemonade stand is a wonderful introduction to entrepreneurial success. When we introduce and teach entrepreneurship, we are preparing the next generation of leaders.

Here's how to teach your child about entrepreneurship using a Lemonade Stand:

Game Plan Process: Teach your children how to turn a general idea into a specific idea by asking questions like:

- What is the product or service?
- Who is going to buy it?
- Where will the location be?

- What are the hours of operation?

- Why do you want to do this?

- How will you get paid?

Answering these questions provides clarity and is an excellent way to begin the process of setting up a Lemonade Stand.

In the brainstorming stages, you are teaching kids how to make their ideas become reality. The "who, what, where, when, why and how" process forms a strategy for the child's business plan. It also teaches them the importance of accountability.

Recruiting Help: The Lemonade Stand activity, teaches valuable life skills. When a child is taught how to shake a person's hand and introduce themselves, they are learning a valuable skill. No matter how you look at it, we are all recruiters. Meeting and playing with our cousins, is recruiting. Meeting people at events outside the home, is recruiting. Making friends, is recruiting. Asking volunteers to play with them is recruiting. Asking an adult to help grab something out of reach, is recruiting. The most important skill to teach a child is to be assertive.

Share an exciting story. Have you ever heard the saying: "Facts tell, stories sell?" Kids love to tell stories about the things they experience. They do it with a great deal of passion! When kids share stories, they express from the heart through pure, honest, excitement. Everyone wants to help them. When children learn how to tell others what they're doing, they are using public relations, communication, marketing and advertising skills.

Entrepreneurship creates confidence. Who will help with the purchase of products, services, and advertising materials? It begins with a small business loan from you. Teach your children the importance of financing their first entrepreneurial adventure. For example, when borrowing the tables for a Lemonade Stand, have them rent the tables for two dollars each. Then, draw up a legal binding contract.

This is where children can learn about financial management:

<u>Expense</u>: How much is the cost to purchase the materials to create a lemonade stand?
<u>Profit:</u> What are the differences between the purchase price

to set up the lemonade stand and the cost to bring it to market?

Loss: What is the negative difference between the setup price and cost of production?

Charity: Tithing ten percent to charity teaches contribution.

Teaching and showing your children how to organize and identify their business can create tremendous developmental skills that may last a lifetime.

"Focusing on each task individually minimizes the enemy of distraction."
-Crystal Horton

CLEARING THE CLUTTER

For most of us, our favorite belongings are found inside our home. Pictures of family and friends adorn the walls. Furnishings are placed creatively throughout the home, providing comfort. Many of us have fond memories of walking into our new home for the first time as a family. Memories of our children rolling over for the first time, giggling, crawling or walking can evoke many warm feelings within the walls of our home.

Sometimes our home become cluttered. Because of our hectic lifestyles things may start to pile up. I recently sat down at my writing desk and realized that it had become a "collection zone" for anything and everything. Some of the items blanketing my desk included: toys, frames that needed to be updated with new pictures, papers to be filed, bills to be paid, brochures from a business I was in seven years ago, old business cards, a sewing machine with fabric for a DIY project and lastly, burlap used for making holiday wreaths for family and friends.

Yes, my desk had evolved from a burgundy, bold and beautiful piece of furniture into a storage bin with no room for a laptop, pen or journal. I felt disempowered sitting at my desk. In front of me were many of the projects I hadn't finished. This could be why I was experiencing writer's block.

One afternoon, while reading a chapter from Stephen Kings Memoir on Writing, I realized that all this clutter was crowding my thoughts. I was creating avoidance strategies that were keeping me from doing the things I loved to do. I recognized that something needed to be done, a drastic change was in order.

So here is what I did.

1. The toys to "look at when I write" were donated.
2. I delegated the frames that needed new pictures to a member of our family who enjoys doing this task.
3. Another task I delegated were papers that needed filing electronically and shredded.
4. I paid bills and then set them up on auto deduct.
5. I threw away brochures and old business cards from the business I closed years ago.
6. The sewing machine with fabric well, I had to face it and admit this was something I was never

going to do, I donated it.

7. I also delegated the DIY wreath project to my creative kid's who actually enjoy making them.

...and just like that, my desk was free of clutter. By clearing the clutter and becoming more efficient with a productively organized system, my mind body and spirit felt cleansed as well.

Below are 3 action steps for clearing clutter:

DECIDE to become more efficient and respectful of your time. Understand the importance of minimizing unnecessary clutter.

DELEGATE to those in the household who might enjoy the project. My obsession with perfection is why I took control of the DIY project and hoarded it on my desk. I let go of my attachment and delegated the project to someone who truly enjoyed it.

DONATE what is not being used and taking up unnecessary space.

Feeling lighter and inspired, I realized my desk was taking

up space and only collecting unnecessary projects. I rarely wrote at my desk and decided to store it in the garage. That space is now clean, clear and organized, adorned with a beautifully decorated small coffee table and chair and picture frames line the walls. This space is now my favorite place to write.

THE IMPORTANCE OF BEING PREPARED

Procrastination is the number one thief of goals. The top reasons for procrastination include, feeling overwhelmed, confusion, boredom, lack of motivation and distractions. Procrastination is not always due to laziness, but to emotional and psychological barriers. It's important to become aware of your procrastination triggers before they can be defeated.

Jillian Michaels, a personal trainer and author of Unlimited, describes boredom as "an inability to feel you're hiding your feelings." For example, when washing the dishes I procrastinate out of boredom. I disconnect from my feelings which creates a lack of motivation. Distractions become my enemy and I may put off washing dishes for a couple of hours. My procrastination may become the example I set for my children who may in turn repeat the same cycle.

Christi Youd, President of Organize Enterprise, LLC, states that "time management is a principle that impacts children's emotional, social, physical, mental, financial and spiritual lives." Productivity organizes an individual's thoughts, allowing the ability to manage larger tasks.

Accomplishing tasks empowers us to keep moving forward with confidence. Setting the example of taking responsibility shows children how to take pride in their work.

Productive time management is a learned behavior that becomes easier through consistent practice. Consider creating a family command center. A family command center is simple to put together and helps decrease procrastination. A command center includes sections on a wall, split into different organized sections. Sections include, the master calendar, chores chart, dinner menu, coupons, receipts, and invoices. This example is an excellent way to teach children how to manage their time.

The distinction between what is urgent and what is important becomes clear through effective time management. Not everything is equally important but by utilizing the family command center as a tool you provide an opportunity for children to learn how to evaluate their options.

Selecting three top priorities to accomplish during the day turns a to-do list from an overwhelming task into an achievement. If a task takes more than 30 minutes, break it up into smaller tasks. The smaller the task, the more likely your child will complete it.

Start each day with the most urgent task and then move to the next. Focusing on each task individually minimizes the enemy of distraction. The confusion of how to move forward often comes from being inadequately prepared. Having a routine set in place is an important component of a family's rhythm. If parents don't promote good habits, their children may spend the rest of their lives trying to get rid of bad habits. Teaching children to conquer their confusion of tasks can prevent crippling effects of anxiety and stress. Kids (and adults) thrive when they are prepared.

A master calendar keeps the family communication channels open. With doctor visits, dentist appointments, play dates, after school activities, sports games, practice schedules, etc., the master calendar becomes the gatekeeper of the household. "Over-scheduling" is minimized. Assign a different color to each family member and over time, the ability to achieve family balance will be reflected in the master calendar.

My mom taught me when a person is late, it's because they don't respect the other person's time. I teach my children this important value when it comes to time management. Teaching good habits comes from preparation. It's never too late to teach children how to organize and prioritize their day. Mastering the tasks of each day will produce a successful week.

CREATE CONSISTENT HABITS

Recently, I overheard some parents contemplating whether a structured routine was necessary for their young child. They felt it didn't allow their child to create and think on his own. I believe children thrive in a structured environment. For example, when a child learns to brush their teeth they're learning good hygiene habits.

Lincoln Chaffee, the seventy-fourth governor of Rhode Island, believes "trust is built with consistency." The more consistent our child becomes the more responsibility we trust them with. A habit is formed by repeating the same structured daily routine. Habits create an internal alarm clock that reminders us to repeat the same actions. This is true of both good and bad habits.

When a parent is an effective role model, children tend to follow their guidance. Creating a structured routine early in a child's life provides consistent behaviors as they move into adulthood. The bonus of teaching consistency early on is that it also helps prepare them to learn how to receive instruction from school teachers.

In our family, when we are facing a challenge to stay consistent here is what we have learned:

Habits form because of a decision made internally. We reflect on why the decision was made, write it down and review our decisions on a regular basis, especially during times of weakness. This can help bring the focus back. For example, when teaching a child to brush their teeth you can create a chart and check mark their daily activity.

It takes time to form a consistent habit. Typically it takes a minimum of 30 days to create a new habit, one that sticks and stays. Teaching children to brush their teeth on a daily basis requires a parent, to become the child's accountability partner.

When learning something new, embrace mistakes. Recognize mistakes as being crucial in the learning process. If your child forgets to brush their teeth, point it out and encourage them to learn the lesson and move on.

Celebrate the small steps. For example, a week has passed, and your child has brushed consistently all week. Celebrate the small steps to get to the big steps.

Some questions to consider:

- As a parent, how do you stay consistent?
- What are some excuses that may be holding you back?
- Do these excuses help you avoid consistency?

Consistency takes practice and patience. Parenting with consistency is the key to a healthy relationship with your child. Consistent behaviors in parenting will create a better understanding of where you and your child stand.

IS YOUR TV BROKEN?

During a recent play date, my daughters' friend asked her, "what's wrong with your TV? Where is the sound? What's wrong with the picture?" My daughter responded, "oh, that thing, we only turn it on in the evening." Her friend responded with a gasp and said, "It's off?" She looked at us as if there was something wrong with us.

Parenting in today's technology driven world can be challenging. There are many high-tech options available, some helpful, some addictive and some seem to serve no purpose at all. We have a choice. We can choose to use today's high-tech world as a learning tool.

I have observed that when my children are acting obnoxious and yelling at each other it's usually a reaction to something they've seen on TV. From one show, the girls seemingly learned that sisters argue and compare. That is how they began treating each other. I routinely found myself acting as the referee. Once I became aware of the behavior patterns influenced by the show my children were watching, my husband, and I made a decision to limit our high-tech influences in the home. Today we are very selective regarding the quality and quantity of the TV shows we watch.

Ultimately our decision was based on the fact that we have a choice. The TV could be our family influence or we, as parents, could. It took about a month to wean our children from TV. In a short time, we recognized the difference in our home. The kids played differently with each other, the respect and care for each other returned. Our family became active. We purchased bikes and joined the YMCA. Today, our choices reflect our lifestyle. We believe that our choices will have a positive impact on our family.

This example illustrates how becoming united as a family can remove negative influences from a home. Our family is united in a positive way. The decisions we make influences our children.

Below are three helpful strategies for parenting in today's high-tech world:

1. Evaluate and modify TV time as needed.
2. Determine what TV shows influence the home.
3. Make a decision whether or not this is in alignment with the family mission statement.

"By depositing something positive into someone else's bucket, we are not only filling their bucket but ours as well.

-Crystal Horton

PEN PALS

In school, our kids are learning how to fill each other's (invisible) bucket. They are learning how to make friendships through love, honor, and respect. By building friendships this way and filling each other's bucket, a long lasting, supportive friendship emerges.

For as long as I can remember, we visited my grandparents on a weekly basis. My brother and I enjoyed building a friendship with our grandparents by eating ice cream, reading books, playing and running in their yard. As my brother and I grew up, our grandparents grew with us. We went from eating ice cream as kids to talking about challenges at school, religion, marriage and parenting tips. Each week our bond grew stronger!

A few years ago my "Grandpo" began struggling with hearing loss. I found myself feeling distant from him because I didn't know how to communicate without raising my voice. My children were growing up and experiencing life, and I wanted to share all the details with Grandpo. I prayed for an answer, for a way to continue our friendship. Sitting across the table from him, seeing him and not being able to talk was agonizing.

One evening, I had an idea. I could start writing letters to my Grandpo. I knew that he loved to receive letters in the mail. I sat down and wrote a letter. From that moment on he was happy and he shared his letters with others. As we continued to visit him each week, he would ask yes and no questions that made him feel like he was part of the conversation again. Through this process, he was able to build a great friendship with my children, who have given him a nickname and write him letters to this day.

We all carry around an invisible bucket containing our feelings. When our bucket is empty, we feel sad. By depositing something positive into someone else's bucket, we not only fill their bucket but ours as well. As parents, we must share this concept with our children. At times, we may feel underappreciated by our children. By reconnecting and growing with other adults, we teach our children how to fill their buckets with a peaceful understanding while also filling up our own.

Do you have a meaningful friendship with a family member? How do you communicate? Have you become distant? What can you do to become close again? Whose bucket can you begin filling today?

MY FINAL LETTER TO "GRANDPO"

Dear Grandpo,

Today I stood at your coffin. With tears in my eyes, I thought of the time you chased the ice cream truck down the street, so "we could enjoy a popsicle together on a hot sunny day." I chuckled at the thought of how you and Grandma would play favorites with me, my brother, and our cousins. I smiled in humble gratitude thinking about the one dollar bets you and Grandma would make over baseball games.

Remembering when you nicknamed me "Ojos de Capulin" is a feeling of pride I will never forget. When you enter the gates of heaven, I image you shaking hands with your fellow soldier buddies, please tell them thank you for me. My freedom to raise my family, write this book and share your story would not be possible without the men and women who have died for our rights, served our country and continue to serve today.

Thank you Grandpo!
Stars and stripes forever,
Ojos de Capulin

TRIBUTE TO ARMED FORCES

My freedom to raise my children, write this book and share my journey with you would not be possible without the men and women who have served and died for our country.

The mental, physical and spiritual training that a soldier endures serving our country is not only brave but heroic. The willingness to face agony, pain, danger, uncertainty and intimidation is courageous.

Thank you to the men and women of the armed forces, their families and loved ones for the sacrifices they make to protect our freedom and secure our nation.

In the next few pages, I want to share a few memories my Grandpo wrote about during his service in World War II.

JOSE LUCRECIO BACA
WORLD WAR II VETERAN

I served my country during World War II as a Corporal in the United States Army.

Inducted into the Service on July 20, 1944, I was sent to Ft. Bliss, Texas for two months and then to Camp Roberts, California for basic training. Soon after that, I was scheduled for overseas duty. I departed from VanCouver, Washington on a ship called "Bosque." Within two days, we were in Saipan. We formed the 23rd replacement depot. We took more combat training there, and a month later I received my orders to be shipped to Okinawa.

On May 1, 1945, we were fighting on the front lines. We were the 96th Infantry Division; we had replaced the 77th Division. Ten days later, our Commander told us that from now on, we were on our own. We were told to take care of ourselves. I was in the Second Squad 1st Platoon, 381st Infantry Regiment.

My friend, Ignacio Baca, and I made a pact. We promised each other that if one of us were wounded, the other would carry him out of the battlefield. On the first day, Ignacio was wounded in combat. The medics got him out, and I never saw him again.

The next day, we continued to fight the enemy. They were waiting for us in foxholes. I used all my ammunition on that first day and had to get more the following day to continue. After that, we went on recognizance patrol. The Japanese opened fire on us, and we immediately jumped into ditches full of water to escape enemy fire. We lost a lot of soldiers that day.

The next day we were able to advance, but we were under heavy enemy fire from all over. We were running to ditches to escape being shot. That same day, our artillery mistakenly sent short rounds of fire at us. They thought we were the enemy. We lost much of the 2nd squad that day from enemy fire as well as friendly fire.

On the 11th of June 1945, we were headed toward a mountain called "Big Escarpment," but before we got there, we had to get through a village full of Japanese soldiers. As we advanced out of the village, about 1000 yards, I was shot in my left shoulder. I told my squad leader that I had been shot; he told me, "Stay down before they shoot you again!'"

Later that day, as I was walking out of the jungle, I encountered one of my buddies. He thought I was Japanese, and he pointed his rifle at my head. He was just about ready to fire when he recognized me. He said, "Oh, Joe, I almost got you, thank God I recognized you in time."

I went to the First Aid Station for one day then I was flown to Guam Hospital to have the bullet removed from my shoulder. I was there for about two months. Then I was flown back to Saipan. I was assigned to AAA USAFI (United Stated Armed Forces Institute). There I supervised the work of 5 Japanese prisoners of war in a warehouse loading and unloading trucks with cargoes of books and other information and educational materials. We used hand trucks, hooks and hydraulic lifts in this work.

A lot of tragic things happened during the war. I will tell you of a few incidents that I remember:

There were many caves for the enemy to hide in. One day as we approached such a cave, we were being shot at by a sniper. One of our men spotted the sniper and shot him, so we were able to advance. As we got closer to the cave, my commander asked a volunteer to secure the cave. I don't know why, but I volunteered. I crawled toward the cave, and when I got close enough, I pulled the pin on a hand grenade and threw it in the cave. No one came out, and when we searched the cave, no one was in it.

Later on, as we proceeded, we were once again faced with a cave. I was going to throw another grenade inside to make sure the enemy was not in there waiting for us. I pulled the pin and was about to throw it in the cave when I saw what looked like a bald head of an old man. I yelled at him to run from the cave. As he walked out with his hands over his head, about ten other civilians followed him, men women and children. I yelled at them to hurry I had my finger covering the hole where I had pulled the pin on the grenade. My commander yelled at me to get rid of the grenade. There was a hole nearby where a telephone pole had previously been. I threw the grenade in the hole and ran for cover. None of us was injured, thank God.

Another incident that I will never forget is the time we were camped out on the border of a nearby ditch. It was dark, and we could hear voices. We spotted a group of people walking toward us. The commander told us to hold our fire until they got closer. When they got about 50 feet from us, we were given the order to fire. The crowd of people included Japanese soldiers as well as civilian men and women. Many of them were killed, and some were wounded. As they screamed and cried for help, it seemed like the end of the world for me. All I could do was pray and ask God for mercy. The next day, we took them to the nearest First Aid Station.

After that, I was sent to Malacca Islands to disarm the enemy. We replaced the 111th Infantry that had been stationed there for a year and had not been involved in combat. Our Infantry had been in combat, and many of us were still recovering from injuries, but we accepted our orders, and we did not question our commander.

Then I was sent back to Saipan. We were camped near the beach when we got word over the radio, which a big wave of water was coming towards us, and we should get out as soon as possible. We took Japanese, eight men to a jeep, and we headed to a cave in the mountains. That night as we settled in, a few of us prayed the rosary out loud in Spanish. The next day our Anglo comrades remarked that we sure talked a lot during the night!

On August 6, 1945, the United States dropped the atomic bomb about 18,000 feet over the Japanese city of Hiroshima. On August 9, 1945, another bomb was dropped on the city of Nagasaki. The bombs devastated both cities. About 70,000 people died at Hiroshima, and about 40,000 at Nagasaki and many more were injured. Within days, the war was over.

I became eligible for discharge and on August 13, 1946, I was discharged from Camp Beale, California.

In conclusion, I pray for our military, our nation and world peace.

Jose Lucrecio Baca

ABOUT THE AUTHOR

I enjoy helping families manage their time, resources and patience while bringing the joy back into parenting. My mission is to help families overcome their biggest challenges.

I believe a family that plays together stays together. Whether it's playing basketball, a board game, reading together, going on a hike, cooking dinner together, yard work, etc..

As a Family Strategist, my creative, energetic strategies are designed to help promote a greater sense of purpose while opening deeper levels of communication within the family unit.

Rather than surviving begin thriving!

www.CrystalHorton.com
BeInspired@crystalhorton.com

ORDER ADDITIONAL COPIES
STRETCH MARKS by Crystal Horton

To order additional copies of this book go to
www.CrystalHorton.com/stretch-marks/

Download this complimentary family planner to help keep
your priorities in order
www.CrystalHorton.com/family-planner

RESOURCES

John Page Burton
Author of Wisdom Through Failure and Knowing Sh#t
from Shinola
www.JohnPageBurton.com

Stan Holden, The Looney Bin Creative Agency
Stretch Marks Book Cover Design
www.TheLooneyBin.com

Dr. Denny Coates
Parenting Author, The Race Against Time
Blog article: The Listening Moment & The Listening
Mindset
http://www.drdennycoates.com/the-listening-moment-the-listening-mindset/

Daren Hardy
Founder of Success Magazine
www.DarrenHardy.com

Jillian Michaels
Author of Unlimited and personal trainer
www.JillianMichaels.com

Helen Williams
Parent counselor and family educator
Blog article "Overprotective Parents? Is this your parenting style?"http://www.consistent-parenting-advice.com/overprotective-parents.html

Hunter Maats and Katie O'Brien
Authors of Straight-A Conspiracy. Blog article "Teaching Students to Embrace Mistakes"
http://www.edutopia.org/blog/teaching-students-to-embrace-mistakes-hunter-maats-katie-obrien

Dr. Anne Dunnelwood
PH.D a licensed psychologist and author of Even June Cleaver Would Forget the Juice Box
Blog article by Kate Bayless.
What is Helicopter Parenting:
http://www.parents.com/parenting/better-parenting/what-is-helicopter-parenting/

Karen Ruskin
Psy.D., author of The 9 Key Techniques for Raising Respectful Children Who Make Responsible Choices
Blog article written by Alonna Friedman, a freelance writer and mother of two
9 Tips for Teaching Kids Responsibility:
https://www.care.com/a/9-tips-for-teaching-kids-responsibility-1303120948

Amy McCready
Founder of Positive Parenting Solutions
Author, "If I Have to Tell You One More Time...The
Revolutionary Program That Gets Your Kids to Listen
Without Nagging, Reminding or Yelling."
Blog Article: How To Teach Kids To Say Sorry
http://www.positiveparentingsolutions.com/parenting/how-to-teach-kids-to-say-sorry

Renee Jain
Chief Storyteller at GoZen.com, Anxiety Relief Programs
for Kids
Blog Article: Help Your Kids Avoid the Indecision Blues
http://www.huffingtonpost.com/renee-jain/help-your-kids-avoid-the-indecision-blues_b_4064633.html

GreatSchools.org
Blog Article: Finding balance in your child's life by
"GreatSchools Staff" Content provided by: PTO Today
http://www.greatschools.org/gk/articles/finding-balance-in-childs-life/

Steve Handel
Psychology Journalist and Self-Improvement Writer
The Emotion Machine
Blog Article "How to Become a Master of Nonverbal
Communication." *http://www.theemotionmachine.com/how-to-become-a-master-of-nonverbal-communication*

Roger Collantes
Author of "Beyond Survival: How To Thrive Amidst Life's Inevitable Crisis"
Blog Article (Inquirer.net): 90 percent of a child's brain development happens before age 5
http://lifestyle.inquirer.net/206697/90-percent-of-a-childs-brain-development-happens-before-age-5#ixzz3rJMizLiw

L.R. Knost
Award-Winning, International Best-Selling Author; Founder & Director of Little Hearts/Gentle Parenting Resources
www.littleheartsbooks.com

Lincoln Chaffee
74th Governor of Rhode Island
Author, "Against The Tide"

Mimi Doe
Author, "Busy but Balanced: Practical and Inspirational Ways To Create a Calmer, Closer Family"
http://www.mimidoe.presskit247.com/

Stephen King
Author, "On Writing: A Memoir of the Craft"

Christi Youd
President, Organize Enterprise, LLC.
Blog Article: Don't Procrastinate! Teach Your Child Time Management
http://www.education.com/magazine/article/Dont_Procrastinate_Teach_Your/

Thomas Winterman
Author, "The Thrive Life"
Blog Article: A Child Therapists perspective on spanking
http://psychcentral.com/blog/archives/2015/09/22/a-child-therapists-perspective-on-spanking/

Raina Telgemeier
Author, Smile
http://goraina.com/books_smile.html

Natalie Angier
Author and Pulitzer-prize winning science columnist for the New York Times
Blog Article: The Changing American Family
http://www.nytimes.com/2013/11/26/health/families.html?pagewanted=all&_r=1